THE ISLAND NATION

THE ISLAND NATION

A History of Britain and the Sea

Brian Lavery

Foreword by Ellen MacArthur

CONWAY
MARITIME PRESS

NATIONAL
MARITIME
MUSEUM

visit Britain

SeaBritain
2005

Author's Acknowledgements

Thanks are due to the staff of the Picture Library at the National Maritime Museum, especially Lucy Waitt and David Taylor; to Library and Manuscripts staff, especially Jill Davies and Daphne Knott; to the Research team, including Nigel Rigby and Janet Norton; to the staffs of the National Archives and London Library; to John Lee and Alison Moss at Conway Maritime Press; to the Publishing Department, headed by Rachel Giles; and to many fellow researchers and the students of the Open Museum who have helped me form ideas over the years. A work like this is only possible because of great advances in British maritime history and archaeology over the last few decades, for which the Society for Nautical Research and publishers like Conway Maritime Press can take much of the credit.

Thanks also to Sarah and Alice Lavery for support and encouragement.

Publisher's Acknowledgements

The publisher would additionally like to thank the following people: Michael Dewing, Deirdre Livingstone at SeaBritain 2005, Jane Collinson at VisitBritain, Stephen Riley at the National Maritime Museum, Jeremy Harrison at the Chamber of Shipping, John Bagnall at the RYA, and Ellen MacArthur.

www.nmm.ac.uk
www.visitbritain.com
www.seabritain.co.uk
www.chrysalisbooks.co.uk

Text © National Maritime Museum, 2005
Volume © Conway Maritime Press, 2005
Gazetteer © British Tourist Authority (trading as VisitBritain), 2005

First published in 2005 by
Conway Maritime Press
The Chrysalis Building
Bramley Road
London W10 6SP

An imprint of Chrysalis Books Group plc

British Library Cataloguing in Publication Data
A record of this title is available from the British Library

ISBN 1 84486 016 7

Editor: Alison Moss
Interior design and layout: Champion Design
Jacket Design: Lee May Lim

Printed in China

JACKET

Front cover (clockwise from top): The Seven Sisters cliffs on the East Sussex coast; *Horatio, Viscount Nelson*, by William Beechey, 1801; *Building the Steamship Great Eastern* by William Parrott, 1858. Spine: The seal of the Cinque Port of Winchelsea. Back cover (from left): *Masters of the Sea: First Battle Cruiser Squadron, 1915*, by William L Wyllie; yachts racing on the Solent; *Robin Hood's Bay* by Richard Eurich.

HALF TITLE PAGE

The Barque Birkdale View from Aft the Bowsprit by Herbert Barnard John Everett.

FRONTISPIECE

View of the castle on Holy Island.

Contents

SeaBritain 2005 is a year-long festival to celebrate Britain's long love affair with the sea, inspired by the bicentenary of Admiral Lord Nelson's famous victory at Trafalgar and his death in action. As an island, and as a nation of seafarers, the sea has shaped, and continues to shape, our history and our culture.

More than 600 festivals, exhibitions and events across the UK will commemorate the bicentenary and celebrate the many ways the sea has an impact on all our lives – as our defence in time of war and our trading link with the world; as a rich source of food and natural resources; the coast as a magnet for tourists; the challenge of sailing and watersports, and the sea as an inspiration for countless generations of artists, musicians and writers.

SeaBritain 2005 is an initiative led by the National Maritime Museum, Greenwich, in partnership with leading national and regional bodies, including VisitBritain, the Official Nelson Commemorations Committee, Royal Navy, RNLI, National Trust, Royal Yachting Association, Sea Vision UK and many, many others – with support from the Department for Culture, Media and Sport.

Other Partners in the SeaBritain 2005 campaign

BBC Coast
Bonhams
British Marine
 Federation
British Waterways
Clipper Ventures
Coast Magazine
English Heritage
Environment Agency
Historic Dockyard
 Chatham
Hotelpacc
International Festival
 of the Sea
Jubilee Sailing Trust
Maritime and
 Coastguard Agency
Maritime London
Marine Conservation
 Society
Marine Society
Met Office
National Boat Shows
National Trust
New Trafalgar
 Dispatch
Northern Ireland
 Tourist Board
Ocean Youth Trust
Ordnance Survey
Passenger Shipping
 Association
Royal Naval Museum
RSPB
Sea Cadets
Seafarers UK
SeaFish
SeaGuernsey
Sea Trade
Society for Nautical
 Research
Tall Ships Youth Trust
The 1805 Club
The Chamber of
 Shipping
The Nelson Society
The New Trafalgar
 Trust Ltd
The Trafalgar Weekend
Trinity House
UK Hydrographic
 Office
Visit London
VisitScotland
Wales Tourist Board
Woodland Trust

LEFT
The Battle of Trafalgar, 21 October 1805, with Nelson's flagship, HMS *Victory* in the centre, by J M W Turner.

Foreword

I have loved the sea since I can remember and have been fascinated by those who attempted such great adventures and magnificent achievements. I can still see myself sat in my school library lost in books describing Sir Francis Chichester's adventures around the world. I really could not get enough of the stories; I could not wait to get out and experience them for myself. From my first time in a boat I was hooked. There is nothing as calming and enthralling as being out on the water, whether it is in the Solent or the middle of the Southern Ocean. This year is a real opportunity for the people of Britain to get out to events or maybe even participate on the water as we celebrate the sea with SeaBritain 2005. As a nation we have an immediate link to the sea and a great historical relationship with it, from the great ships such as HMS *Victory*, through to the formula one racing yachts that we see battle away on the water today. I hope that this year will inspire everyone in whatever way possible to take part in this great event. Go and see the ships from the past, visit your local maritime museum, get out on the water and have a go. It might just be the start of things for the next great explorer or racer!

Ellen MacArthur

Ellen MacArthur
Skipper, B&Q trimaran

Chapter 1
The British Seas

The Origin of Britain

Great Britain became an island around 6,500 BC, when the seas finally broke through the chalk hills and created the Strait of Dover which separates England and France. The landmass had been formed many millions of years before. It had been covered with an ice sheet north of the Thames and Severn valleys during the great Ice Age which had ended about 3000 years earlier. The melting ice had flooded much of the land to give Britain a shape not unlike that familiar to us today, although with many detailed differences. The new island was sparsely populated and on the fringe of European society. It would be many millennia before it would have much impact on the rest of the world.

The British Seas

Britain is washed by four main seas, each leading in a different direction and with its own geography. The North Atlantic is by far the largest, and has a fearsome reputation as a wide and stormy ocean. Unlike other oceans its islands are mostly round the edges rather than in the middle, so it has to be crossed in one go. Its waves break dramatically on the west coast of Britain, causing delight with surfers but trepidation among seafarers. But for more than 500 years the Atlantic has provided Britain with its main route to the outside world beyond Europe. Britain's position has also allowed her

to interrupt the worldwide trade of other nations such as the Netherlands and Germany.

The North Sea is very different. It is much shallower and narrower than the Atlantic, although it is not immune from rough weather. In contrast with the rocky Atlantic coast, the North Sea coastline has low cliffs, beaches and numerous sandbanks. It has been the route for many invasions of Britain, including the Vikings and the Anglo-Saxons. It has carried trade to Germany and Scandinavia, and along its shores in the form of coal from north-east England to London. It has seen much warfare between the British and the Dutch and Germans. It has also provided more natural resources than any of the other British seas. In the eighteenth and nineteenth centuries it was one of the world's greatest sources of fish. Since the twentieth it has supplied oil and gas.

The English Channel is, in a sense, the defining feature of Britain, making it an island. The Channel has served as a barrier to invasion and immigration, but it operates equally well as a trade route, with ships passing across it, and just as many going along it and bringing the wealth of the world to northern Europe.

The Irish Sea is the smallest. It is the meeting place of several different cultures – Welsh, Scottish, Irish, Northern Irish, Lancastrian and Manx. It provides the sea routes to the great ports of Glasgow and Liverpool.

Mainland Britain is an island more than 600 miles long, almost entirely situated between latitude 50° and 60° North. It is more than 300 miles wide between Pembrokeshire and Norfolk, and only about 40 miles wide at its narrowest point between the Firths of Clyde and Forth. England, Scotland and Wales have 22.7 million hectares of land, including offshore islands.

Britain's position in the world has given her certain advantages as a trading and maritime power. She is well situated for communication with most of northern Europe and has constantly interacted with its culture and economy. Britain also looks the other way across her Atlantic coast. The great ocean can take her

ships to North America, and this has played a key role in British and world history. It can also carry them to the other great seas of the world – the Caribbean, the Mediterranean, the Indian and the Pacific Oceans, where the British traded, colonised and settled.

Tides and Winds

Few countries have such strong tides as Britain, where the great mass of water from the Atlantic is funnelled into channels and estuaries. The tides are a trap for the unwary, but a skilful sailing-ship navigator can use them to his advantage even when winds are unfavourable or light. They are far more predictable than winds and a sailor can calculate exactly when the tide will carry him up the River Thames or down the English Channel.

Britain has been described as a climatic battleground, with weather coming from four main directions: Tropical Maritime bringing warm, wet weather from the south, Tropical Continental bringing warm, dry air, Polar Maritime with wet, cold air and Polar Continental with cold, dry conditions. Its weather, however, is dominated by the depressions that form well out into the Atlantic and sweep across the country bringing rain and strong winds. The south westerly wind is most common, but far from universal. The weather was largely unpredictable to the ancient seaman, and even the modern forecaster often finds it hard to give a detailed report. But variations in winds can also be an advantage. Almost any wind can be found if the sailor is able to wait for it, which allowed a very varied pattern of trade under sail.

Britain has a temperate climate, experiencing few of the extremes that can disrupt trade in other parts of the world. The sea never freezes and devastating storms such as hurricanes are very rare. The Gulf Stream carries warm water across the Atlantic from the Gulf of Mexico and gives the country warmer temperatures than its latitude would suggest; Glasgow, for example, is further north than Moscow. Britain's climate may mean more rainfall, but this is no problem for the hardy seafarer.

The Coastline

Britain has a great variety of coastline. In the west it is mainly mountainous and rocky, with numerous islands, sea lochs, inlets and rocks washed by the storms of the Atlantic. It has very strong tides and currents – the Bristol Channel has the third highest tidal range in the world, with a rise and fall of up to 13 metres, while the Scottish islands have the famous whirlpool of Corryvreckan. The central part of the coast is protected by Ireland from the effects of the Atlantic. The water is not very deep until 50 to 100 miles out when the continental shelf ends, and it falls steeply to 4000 metres in the south-west. In places the coast has very wide and quite dangerous beaches, such as Morecambe Bay. Its estuaries provide the sites for the great ports of western trade – Bristol, Cardiff, Liverpool and Glasgow. Each of these ports was sited because of its good hinterland rather than easy navigation, and each needed a great deal of highly advanced civil engineering work to make it successful.

The east coast is generally flatter and straighter than the west, and more sheltered from the worst of the gales. It has many sand-banks in the south, but few rocks. The sea in the area is never more than 200 metres deep and provides excellent fishing grounds. It does not have many islands, and even some of these have joined the mainland. Thanet, in the north-east corner of Kent, is still known as an island, although it ceased to be one more than 500 years ago. The coastline has many cliffs, often caused by coastal erosion, and just as many flat beaches. It has several very important estuaries. The Thames leads up to London, and the estuary formed a strong maritime region of its own in the days of Thames sailing barges. The Forth almost cuts Scotland in two and most of the great land battles between England and Scotland were fought near its banks. The building of the great railway bridge 9 miles west of Edinburgh in 1890 was a major feat of civil engineering.

The south coast has many indentations, but it is relatively straight in its general trend from east to west. This gave it a great advantage over the French coast, which has far deeper bays. It was relatively easy to pass from one English headland to another, and north European shipping tended to follow that route to and from the Atlantic, perhaps stopping at English ports for shelter or replenishment. It has very few rocks, compared with French Brittany for example, and these tend to be prominent and easy to avoid, such as the Great Mewstone off Plymouth. It has few offshore sandbanks that are dangerous to shipping, until one approaches the Strait of Dover in the east and is almost in the North Sea. Many natural harbours were formed as the ice melted and drowned the river valleys, creating broad estuaries and sounds at places such as Plymouth and Falmouth. Harbours like these proved a great strategic advantage to Britain in the wars with France.

The Changing Coastline

Britain's coastline is more than 6000 miles long. It is slowly but constantly changing; some lands are lost to the sea, others are reclaimed. The most important long-term feature was set in motion by the melting of the ice 10,000 years ago. Since then the island has gradually tilted as the south-east of England sinks at the rate of roughly 2 millimetres per year, and the north-west of Scotland, freed from the great load, gradually rises. This is seen most dramatically in the raised beaches of western Scotland and the Hebrides. Most of the west coast of the island of Jura, for example, forms part of a beach that was once at sea level and is now between 30 and 100 metres above it.

Another significant feature is coastal erosion, which is particularly common in the softer rocks in the south and east. Some of the flooded lands became the stuff of legend. It was said that the Goodwin Sands off Kent were once prosperous farmland, although without any real evidence. The fabled land of Lyonesse lay between Cornwall and the Scilly Isles. But even lands whose existence is far more certain, and which disappeared within recorded history, exercise a great fascination. Dunwich in Suffolk was some distance from the sea

when it was founded in 630 but by 1753 most of its houses and churches were underwater. The city of Kenfig in South Wales flourished around 1280 but was slowly submerged by sand dunes and reduced to a village by 1538. More recently, a sandbank off Start Point in Devon was dredged for shingle in 1897 and, as a result, the village of Hallsands disappeared over the next 20 years.

It is not all loss, and many significant areas have been reclaimed from the sea over the centuries, mostly by human effort. The Wantsum Channel between Thanet and Kent was reclaimed by monks at the end of the Middle Ages. Further south, Romney Marsh gradually emerged during a lowering of the sea level from the eighth century onwards, and was reinforced by sea walls to provide good agricultural land. In Scotland, the banks of the River Clyde were built up in the eighteenth and nineteenth centuries to make Glasgow accessible as a port, incidentally providing the sites for the rise of Clyde shipbuilding.

It is not possible to feel completely safe behind sea walls, as a great flood, which caused many deaths in eastern England and the Thames Estuary, showed in 1953. The Thames Barrier, first used in 1983, continues to protect London and has to be closed far more than was projected. Present-day policy is for 'managed retreat' from untenable lands, and the effects of global warming may also alter the coastline.

The Islands

The British Isles, by definition, includes many islands, many of which are inhabited. When considering them, the boundaries of 'Britain' become blurred. The Isle of Man and the Channel Islands are ruled by the British Crown but not by its Parliament and technically are not part of the country of Britain. Ireland is closely linked with Britain by geography and economics, and politically it shares a rather violent past, but it retained its own culture through centuries of English occupation and the majority of its people opted for independence. Northern Ireland is part of the British state, although this continues to be contested by some.

ABOVE

The Skye Bridge was built
across the Kyle of Lochalsh in
1995 to link the island with the
Scottish mainland. Tolls were
removed at the end of 2004 after
a long campaign.

Some islands are indisputably part of Britain. Sheppey off the coast of Kent is linked by a bridge, as is Skye in the Hebrides and Anglesey off Wales. The Isle of Wight is less than 5 miles from the south coast of England and is linked by constant ferry services. The Scillies, to the west of Cornwall, are further out and have a distinctive, almost Mediterranean, climate.

There are relatively few islands off the east coast. There are several off Essex, all low-lying and close to the shore such as Foulness, and Northey which is cut off only at high tide. One has to travel 200 miles further north to reach the Farne Islands, famous for bird life and Grace Darling, and the even more famous Lindisfarne or Holy Island, which is also only an island at high tide. The Firth of Forth has a few islands, mostly uninhabited and including the Isle of May with its lighthouse and monastery and the volcanic Bass Rock.

The south coast is equally short of islands, apart from Wight, which shelters the ports of Portsmouth and Southampton as well as providing numerous holiday resorts and a great yachting centre. Portland in Dorset is another misnamed island. St Michael's Mount off Cornwall, which forms a pair with the larger Mont St Michel off Brittany, is linked to the mainland by a causeway. The Bristol Channel has several small islands of which Lundy is the best known, while Anglesey, with its famous bridge by Thomas Telford, is by far the largest and best known Welsh one.

On reaching the west coast of Scotland, islands appear in far greater numbers. The inner Hebrides lie mostly close to the mainland. Some, such as Skye, are spectacularly mountainous, while Islay is comparatively flat. The majority are sparsely populated and rely on tourism, agriculture and some whisky distilling for their income. The outer Hebrides form a much more regular chain, starting with Lewis in the North and gradually decreasing in size until Barra Head more than 130 miles to the south.

The Orkney Islands to the north of Scotland are relatively flat. Most of their landmass is grouped round the great natural harbour of Scapa Flow, with an irregular archipelago to the north. Shetland is another 100 miles further north and is much hillier, with the mainland running north to south. The islands are 700 miles from London, about the same distance as Milan or Barcelona.

Coastal Wildlife

British shores accommodate a great variety of wildlife, in rock pools and on cliff faces for example. The beaches so beloved of British holidaymakers support little natural life, except the lugworm, which buries deep into them. Marshlands and cliffs are more heavily populated, with many kinds of bird. The natives of St Kilda in the Outer Hebrides made their living by collecting sea birds' eggs from the cliff faces, and throughout the British Isles birds are a lure to bird-watchers. Perhaps sea birds, with their raucous noises and predatory habits, are not as attractive as the songbirds to be found further inland. Occasionally the huge herring gulls of Cornwall try to snatch fish and chips from peoples' hands, or the terns of the Farne Islands dive-bomb visitors to protect their nests, but gulls are an essential part of the seaside experience. Puffins are among the most attractive of seabirds.

The creatures which live under the sea are far more valuable as a food source, and yet again there is great variety. The oysters of Whitstable were world famous until they were wiped out in the 1950s, but Morecambe Bay shrimps are still harvested. Crabs and lobsters are found in many areas. Salmon can be caught in season in Scottish rivers, but many more are raised in fish farms in lochs and estuaries. Further offshore are the greatest prizes of all – the cod and herring which supported the great fishing industry at the beginning of the twentieth century.

The Island Peoples

Who are the island peoples of Britain? Britain is an island, but it is not quite as simple as that. There never was a time when the boundaries of the state coincided with the island of Britain, even if one ignores the smaller islands such as Wight and the Hebrides. Historically, Britain was divided into many kingdoms, which crystallised into the English, Scots and Welsh before they were united in the Act of Union in 1707. Ireland was included in the Union from 1801. Today Northern Ireland remains part of the United Kingdom (although it is obviously not part of the island of Britain), while Ireland became independent in 1922. Wales and

Scotland now have devolved parliaments, and the growing authority of Europe and the dominance of America have eroded British independence. But for all their differences, the island peoples of Britain became for a while the most successful maritime nation in modern history, creating the largest empire of all time, backed for more than 200 years by the strongest navy and the largest merchant fleet. And Britain is still a maritime nation, though not in the way she once was.

Noel Coward's great naval film *In Which We Serve* concludes with the lines: 'There will always be other ships, for we are an island race'. But why is being an island so important to Britain? It is not just that the British need ships to communicate with their neighbours. Throughout modern history, the British have interacted just as much with America and the Empire as with nearby Europe, and ships would be needed for that anyway. Partly it is because the British, as long as they have a strong navy and economy, have been able to take as much or as little of European affairs as they want to, to avoid the impact of individual totalitarian movements, for example. Just as important, no part of the long, narrow island is more than 80 miles from the sea, and even inland areas are often served by good navigable rivers. In the ages up to the nineteenth century, when sea transport was far more useful than land transport, this gave the country a great advantage. The British coastline is blessed with large and small natural harbours formed by estuaries, bays and sounds. All these advantages gave Britain the motive and the opportunity to become a great maritime power in the days of sail and steam.

BELOW
Lobster pots in the fishing harbour at Pittenweem in Fife. It is still a working harbour, with a fleet of boats and a fish market.

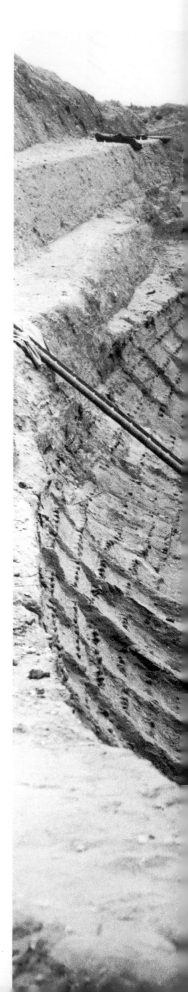

Chapter 2
The Age of Invasions

The Early Britons and the Sea

There is no doubt that the early peoples of Britain were dependent on the sea and used boats, even if few substantial relics of them have been found. There is evidence that they could cross between Britain and Ireland and to offshore islands long before the break with Europe. The earliest evidence of settlement in Scotland is to be found in shell mounds where the people of the tiny island of Oronsay deposited their waste around 5500 years ago. The mainland peoples must have been able to cross the numerous rivers of the area, and to use boats to fish from. They probably had rafts or log boats hollowed out from tree trunks. The Brigg log boat of around 1000 BC was huge, measured 15 metres long, and was perhaps paddled by a large number of men, raising the possibility that it was a ceremonial craft, or the first known British vessel of war. The early peoples may also have used hide boats made from animal skin, a tradition that survived through the ages. Julius Caesar discovered them when he landed in 55 BC, and later adapted them for his own campaigns. They were not light craft like the coracle, but had strong ribs under wickerwork covered with skins, and were large enough to need several men to transport them.

The British peoples began to realise the limitations of the log boat, which in its simple form could never be bigger than the tree from which it was made. There were several ways of dealing with this, but it seems that in Britain the most common solution was to build up the sides with planks, until the original log in the base became less and less important. One early boat, the Brigg 'raft' of about 400 BC, had a flat, square bottom of five planks joined in the same way, with vertical sides and square ends. It was used as a ferry on one of the creeks of the River Humber.

But already the British had discovered how to use the sea. The Dover boat dates from about 1300 BC. Its location, and our knowledge of the existence of trade between Britain and northern France, suggest that it was the first known cross-channel vessel. It was similar to the Ferriby boat in construction, was about 10 metres in length and was paddled by about 18 men.

The Romans

Until this time the British had been on the fringes of the world, though not outside it. They were in regular contact with their Celtic cousins across the Channel in Gaul and as far away as Spain, and were visited by traders from further afield. But they knew very little about the great civilisations of Mesopotamia, Egypt and Greece, which were pushing gradually westwards through the ages. In 55 BC they had their first full-scale encounter with the power of Rome, when Julius Caesar led an expedition to

BELOW
The excavation of the Sutton Hoo boat in 1939, showing the shape of the ribs and planks and the rivets that held them together.

prevent the Britons supporting the conquered Gauls. He landed with two legions near the present town of Deal in Kent, but he was unable to bring cavalry and his ships were almost wrecked in a storm after the landing. The following year he built special shallow-draught craft propelled by sail and oars which could be beached, and landed in the same area with 800 ships, 5 legions and 2000 cavalry. But he did not conquer the country. It was almost a century before a force of 40,000 men under Aulus Plautius landed on the east coast of Kent in AD 43. This time they stayed, and within four years the boundary of the Roman province was defined by the rivers Trent and Severn. They completed Hadrian's Wall by AD 128 and the Antonine Wall, across the narrowest part of Scotland, by AD 142.

The classic Roman warship – the rowing galley with its ram bow, three tiers of oars and a crew of about 100 – was not very suitable for the strong tides and rough seas of northern Europe, as Julius Caesar had recognised. Nevertheless, they set up a fleet, the *Classis Britannica*, based at Dover, and they probably adopted some British practices in their ship design and construction. The fleet employed about 7000 men, mostly of Mediterranean origin. In about AD 82 the Governor Agricola sent an amphibious expedition to the north, with galleys and soldiers. As noted in Tacitus's *Agricola*: 'The war was pushed forward by land and sea; and infantry, cavalry and marines, often meeting in the same camp, would mess and make merry together'. But Britain remained in many ways the remotest point of the Roman Empire. It was closer to Rome than the eastern provinces such as Egypt and Syria, but it was only accessible by travelling over the exposed seas of the region.

Roman Merchant Shipping

The Romans developed a strong trading pattern, with imports including wine, pottery, fruit and marble. They used deep-hulled sailing ships built in the Mediterranean style with a strong frame and planks that were joined edge to edge to create a smooth surface. Unlike the galleys

The Ferriby Boat

THE first of three found on the north bank of the River Humber, the boat known as Ferriby 1 dates between 1390 and 1130 BC. The base is made up of three planks laid side by side. Each has raised projections, carved as part of the plank, with holes in them. Small timbers were passed through the holes and wedged in place to strengthen the joins between the planks, which were also lashed together. The sides were built up by at least two more planks, sewn in place with leather – a common form of construction in societies that used metal sparingly. The gaps between the planks were filled with moss to keep them watertight and wedges were driven in to fill some of the spaces. The Ferriby boat was probably propelled by poles in the shallow water of the Humber Estuary, and by paddles in slightly deeper water. It has been measured as 15.4 metres long and 2.6 metres broad, and she could have carried up to 5.5 tonnes of crew, passengers and cargo as a ferry.

ABOVE
Archaeologists look at the first of the boats to be found in the mud at North Ferriby in the Humber Estuary in 1937.

BELOW
A reconstruction of the Ferriby boat, with known areas in dark wood and more speculative features in a lighter colour.

they could not be drawn up on a beach and needed fairly deep water. Remains found at Blackfriars in the centre of London date from the second century. The ship had a flat bottom and curved sides. The ribs were strong and the planks were laid edge to edge in the Roman fashion, suggesting a combination of the Roman building style with a local hull shape. She was about 16.8 metres long and 6.7 metres broad and had been carrying building stone from the River Medway.

The Romans developed the first real ports, including London (Londinium) on a site on the River Thames with deep water and a crossing point by bridge. York (Eboracum) had its first fort in AD 71, but it was also a major port using the strong tides of the River Ouse. The Romans built up the banks of the river behind wooden walls so that ships could come alongside to unload. However, they were essentially a land people. They built their famous roads and were the first to move through Britain more easily by land than by sea – and in a sense the only ones until the railways were built in the nineteenth century.

By the end of the fourth century the Romans were beginning to feel pressure from the tribes of northern Europe who were migrating westwards. They began to build forts round the 'Saxon shore' in south-east England such as the one at Richborough in Kent. Around 410 the Roman legions were withdrawn to defend Rome from attack by the Goths and the Anglo-Saxons became dominant in England.

The Anglo-Saxons and the Scots

The Anglo-Saxons, who settled in England as the Roman Empire fell into decline, had a very different culture from the Romans. They neglected towns and cities, partly because their boats were smaller and lighter and could be pulled ashore or unloaded in shallow water, so they did not need ports in the usual sense. Their ships were built in the north European tradition, with overlapping planks known as clinker building. The frames were much less important than in the Roman style of building. In the early tenth century the natives of England continued to evolve their own boat-building style. The Graveney boat, recovered from the Kent marshes, has several unique

LEFT
A model of the Roman port of London, showing a ship arriving, the first London Bridge and riverside warehouses.

The Sutton Hoo Boat

IN 1938 archaeologists discovered the outline of a boat in a mound at Sutton Hoo near the town of Woodbridge in Suffolk. The timbers and iron nails had rotted away, but an impression was left in the ground. The site was also filled with goods such as gold and silver ornaments, clothes, weapons and a bronze and iron helmet with face mask.

Though no body was found, it is clear that the site was the commemoration of an Anglo-Saxon chieftain, probably King Raedwald, who ruled East Anglia from 599 until his death in 625. The boat was probably of higher specification than normally used by the Angles and Saxons, but representative of their technology. It would have measured about 27 metres in length, clinker built with nine strakes of plank on each side. The keel on which they were based does not survive. Modern experiments with a half-scale model suggest that it could sail well, with speeds of 10 knots in a 16–18-knot wind. It probably carried about 28 oars, and could be rowed at a speed of about 6 knots.

Artefacts recovered from the Sutton Hoo burial boat include (from top) a bronze and iron helmet, a shield, a purse and a bridle clasp.

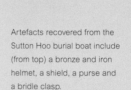

features including the type of nails and the heavy frames, possibly combining Anglo Saxon and native British traditions.

In the north, the Scots, who were originally natives of Ireland, had crossed to Caledonia in skin boats by 500. They were followed by the great Christian missionary Columba, who set up his monastery on the island of Iona in 563 and travelled round the islands and lochs in coracles or curraghs. They were perhaps 4 to 8 metres long, made of leather stretched on a wooden frame, but no hard archaeological evidence of them survives. They could sail quite well with the wind behind them and one once made more than 5 knots between the Sound of Shuna and Iona, but they had little under the water and would be blown sideways or backwards if the wind was ahead.

The Vikings

The British peoples were about to encounter one of the greatest seafaring races of all time. In 793 the great monastery on the island of Lindisfarne was raided by ships and men from the north – the Vikings. Alciun of York described the attack in a letter to the Northumbrian king:

> ...never before has such a terror appeared in Britain as we have now suffered from a pagan race, nor was it thought that such an inroad from the sea could be made. Behold the church of St Cuthbert spattered with the blood of the priest of God, despoiled of its ornaments.

The Celtic monasteries with their island locations were especially vulnerable and Iona was raided in the 790s, along with numerous coastal villages. But despite their initial ferocity, the Norsemen had a strong culture and a well-organised society. Eventually they would convert to Christianity and settle in many parts of Britain.

The origin of the term 'Viking' is far from certain, but the most common view is that it meant a kind of pirate who waited in a *vik* or bay for his prey. The more neutral term 'Norsemen' tells us something about their origin,

in Scandinavia. Pressure of population caused raiding then migration. The Swedes tended to go eastwards down the rivers of Russia, while the Danes moved towards eastern England as the Anglo-Saxons had done several centuries earlier. They conquered and settled most of east-central England, ruling it under Danelaw, by 880. The Norwegians, an Atlantic people themselves, had little to fear from the strong tides and fierce storms of north and west Britain. Orkney, on the fringes of the world for most people, became a crossroads for them, as they ventured out into the Atlantic towards Iceland, Greenland and

BELOW
An Irish fisherman carries a coracle on his back in the 1860s, using a design that has remained unaltered in principle through the centuries.

eventually North America or 'Vineland'. They also moved down the west of Britain, leaving many traces on the Scottish islands, founded the city of Dublin, and settled in north-west England. Another group settled in northern France and became known as the Normans – England would see more of them later.

The Viking ship is well known from almost intact examples found in Norway and Denmark. It was double ended and could sail either way, and was clinker built in the north European tradition. It had a high, curved bow and stern, and was often richly decorated. It had fine lines but was wide at midships to allow it to carry sail when the wind was abeam. Unlike earlier ships seen in Britain it had a deep keel, which prevented it being driven sideways by the wind, and allowed it to be hauled on shore and over land with minimum damage to its bottom. It could be rowed as well as sailed and was large and strong enough to survive the worst weather. As well as the great longships, which were used for warlike purposes, the Norsemen used ships for trade. The knorr was shorter, broader and deeper than the longship, for carrying goods.

One English King who resisted the Vikings was Alfred of Wessex, who reigned from 871 to 899. Most of his defence was by land fortification, but towards the end of his reign he built an English fleet, using larger and higher ships than the Vikings. In 896 they fought a successful battle against the Danes and forced them to retreat to East Anglia. Alfred's successors used their sea power to establish a supremacy over the whole of England until, under Aethelred in the 990s, they were defeated at battles such as Maldon in Essex and had to pay the notorious Danegeld to keep the raiders out of their territory. The Dane Cnut became king of all England in 1016 and ruled well for nearly 20 years. After that the Wessex dynasty was restored in the person of Edward the Confessor. His death in 1066 would precipitate a new crisis.

ABOVE
Two sides of a coin from around 880 in the time of King Alfred, with our only known contemporary image of him.

BELOW
Vikings raiding, as depicted on a stone in the ruined abbey on Lindisfarne Island.

Chapter 3
The Middle Ages

The Norman Invasion

When Edward the Confessor died in 1066, Harold Godwinson, son of the Earl of the West Saxons, assumed the throne. Duke William of Normandy, descended from Norsemen who had settled in northern France, believed that he had a far better claim, and furthermore that Harold had sworn allegiance to him two years earlier.

William built a fleet of 700 ships in the Viking style. The Normans had adopted cavalry as the main means of warfare, and perhaps half William's ships were horse transports, carrying six to eight animals each. They sailed from the River Somme to Pevensey where they landed unopposed – the English fleet was waiting for them at the Isle of Wight 70 miles to the west.

BELOW
Horses are disembarked from Duke William's ships during his invasion of England, as shown by the Bayeux tapestry.

Harold had been distracted by a Norwegian invasion of the north of his country and his army was exhausted after a battle and a long march south. The two armies met north of Hastings on 14 October and Harold was defeated and killed. The Normans took over as a new and highly organised ruling class.

The Normans moved away from their Viking roots as they consolidated their power in England. They became more involved in land warfare and agriculture: seafaring became more of a specialised profession. In theory the seaman was subject to very strict regulation – the Laws of Oleron, for example, proscribed severe punishments for mutiny, theft and piracy. But Draconian regulation is often just a symptom of how hard it is to enforce any kind of rule, and the medieval seaman lived in an anarchic world in which piracy was rife. Feuds between towns could assume the proportions of a small civil war, such as the one between the Cinque Ports and Yarmouth, which lasted nearly a century and led to the destruction of 17 ships in 1303 alone.

The Sea in the Middle Ages

The sea now seemed less important than it had done in the past or would do in the future. The feudal system, as established by the Normans, was based on land tenure rather than moveable wealth. Naval warfare was made as much like land warfare as possible, using the same weapons and with castles built on ships. However, the horse which dominated on land was useless at sea, and transporting them caused special problems – a knight needed at least three horses in support besides the one he rode. The British Isles were not invaded from

BELOW
A fourteenth-century knight in a ship travelling to the Crusades in the Holy Land, with his horse and attendants. The picture makes horse transport look easier than it actually was.

The Newport Ship

THE remains of a ship that were found on the site of a new arts centre on the banks of the River Usk in Newport, Gwent in the summer of 2002 fill a significant gap in British maritime archaeology. They are the best example of a medieval vessel in the country. Some of her timbers have been dated as early as 1427, while others, including the cradle in which she was laid up, are from 1465–7. She is a 'keel' of clinker build with overlapping planks to which an internal frame was added. Her bow and stern have not been recovered but it seems likely that she had high castles. Much of her starboard side is intact. Her measurements are 25 metres long with a beam of about 8 metres. Numerous artefacts such as leather shoes, wooden bowls, gunshot, a comb, gaming counters and barrel staves have been found, providing a picture of the life of the ship.

Research is still in progress, but it seems that she was built between 1427 and 1465. She had returned from a voyage to Spain and Portugal, for her remains contained coins and Portuguese pottery. Possibly she was leaking and was laid up around 1467 in the town's harbour near the castle. A conservation centre is being set up to preserve the remains.

BELOW
Archaeologists work inside the hull of the Newport ship.

---

outside as they had been in the past, although the English launched their invasion of Ireland. There was no overseas empire, and the royal possessions in France needed only short-distance transport.

On the other hand, the Middle Ages saw a revival of the English town after centuries of neglect by the Anglo-Saxons. Towns were about trade, which was best carried by water, especially bulk goods such as coal and timber. Ships were relatively small and the rivers had not yet silted up as they would do in later times, so inland towns, such as York, Stirling, Norwich and Leicester, were served well by rivers. However, the ships of the era were deep-draughted and heavy compared with their Viking predecessors, so they could not be drawn up on a beach and needed real harbour facilities.

Naval Warfare

English kings, unless distracted by war or rebellion, tended to follow expansionist policies in more than one direction. Ships were obviously needed in wars with France or Ireland. When Edward I conquered Wales in the 1280s he built a ring of castles on the north-west coast, all supplied by water, demonstrating how much the English relied on sea power. Conflicts between England and Scotland tended to be fought on land, but an invading army needed to be supplied by sea in an inhospitable country where the Scots operated a scorched earth policy. The classic invasion route, from Berwick to Edinburgh and then Stirling, was well suited to this. When the Scots began to operate their own privateers from the coast of Fife, this strategy became much more difficult for the English and they never did conquer Scotland permanently.

The main task of a naval force was to transport or supply an army, so sea battles were extremely rare, and there were only six fully-fledged ones in more than 500 years. There was no way in which one ship could sink or seriously damage another and the main means of attack was with the land weapons of arrows, lances, maces, etc. A merchant ship became a warship when she took on a company of soldiers, and perhaps had wooden castles built in the bow and stern. The 'captain' of the ship was the leader of the soldiers, the 'master' was the person in charge of navigation. In battle, his role was to bring the ship alongside an enemy one of approximately the same size, leaving the enemy flagship to his own admiral. After that, the soldiers fought the battle. On the whole the English were successful in battle, winning at Damme in 1213, Dover in 1217, Sluys in 1340, Winchelsea in 1350 and Harfleur in 1416. They lost at La Rochelle in 1372. All battles were fought very close to land.

In Scotland, the Lords of the Isles had a different kind of navy. Centred on the island of Islay, the clan Donald had a great deal of independence from the Scottish Crown for about 200 years up to 1498. The clan used a fleet of galleys and birlinns, direct descendants of the Viking longship, to rule the Hebrides and the land nearby. Unlike the English and Scottish kings, they demanded feudal service in the form of ships – the Isle of Man, for example, was held for the service of six galleys of 26 oars each.

British naval forces in the Middle Ages were concerned with home waters and the near continent, with one major exception. In 1190 Richard I travelled overland to Marseilles to join the Third Crusade against the occupation of the Holy Land by the Muslim Saracens. Most of his shipping was hired locally but he also sent a fleet of up to 110 ships, which assembled at Dartmouth. Although he failed to capture Jerusalem, Richard and his seamen learned much about maritime technology, including horse transportation and possibly the use of the compass.

BELOW
This illustration of the Battle of Sluys in 1340 portrays the hand-to-hand fighting that was typical of sea fights of the age.

ABOVE AND RIGHT
The seals of the Cinque Ports of Winchelsea (upper) and Rye (lower). The Winchelsea seal shows a ship with its sails furled and temporary castles built on its bow and stern, with a side rudder. The Rye ship has its sails set with more permanent castles and a stern rudder.

The Rise and Fall of English Navies

Eventually English kings, especially those with the most enemies or the most ambitious foreign policies, outgrew improvised navies and needed more specialised forces. Unpopular at home and with his French possessions under threat, King John (ruled 1199–1216) built up a fleet of more than 50 ships including galleys, but failed to use them effectively. Henry III and Edward III also built substantial but short-lived navies.

The process culminated in Henry V's reign. Pursuing his war with France, as celebrated by Shakespeare in his eponymous play, he had a fleet of 17 ships, 7 carracks, 2 barges and 12 'balingers' by his death in 1420. The largest of these was the great ship the *Grace Dieu* of about 1500 tons, which was built from 2591 oak trees and 1195 beeches in 1418. It would be several centuries before a larger warship appeared in British waters, but she was accidentally burned in 1439 without seeing active service, and the remains can be seen at very low water to this day on the River Hamble.

Trade Routes

The medieval system encouraged a good deal of self-sufficiency within villages and towns, but nevertheless a strong trading community developed in luxury goods such as wine and fine cloth, and in necessities such as furs, hides, coal, timber, salt and metals. Trade was strictly regulated, in theory at least. The Hansa League, founded in Lubeck in the late fourteenth century, dominated much of northern Europe and the Baltic. It had a Kontore or counting house in London, and stations at other ports such as Yarmouth. The trade of each town was controlled by its merchant guild, while the Crown tried to impose customs dues on exports and imports.

In England the Cinque Ports were a powerful body. Originally they consisted of five ports in the south east of England, as their name implies – Sandwich, Dover, Hythe, Romney and Hastings. Others were added as 'incorporated towns' or 'limbs'. They are often seen as a military force but their main obligation, to provide ships of the king's use for 15 days a year, was rarely demanded. They acted as naval advisors to the king and helped ferry his armies to and from his lands in France, and in return they had valuable trading privileges. By 1350 most of the harbours were too shallow to be successful as ports and a few, such as Winchelsea, were eventually left some distance from the sea. Larger ports such as London, Boston and Southampton were flourishing in their place.

The English and Scottish wool industries developed in the twelfth century, and this provided the island's main export commodity, supplying the cloth-makers of the Netherlands and Italy. About 30,000 sacks were exported annually in the middle of the fourteenth century, and England was beginning to develop her own textile industry, so finished cloth was also transported. Other cargoes included coal from the north east of England, and grain when there was a surplus. The main English import was wine from Gascony. It was transported in casks known as 'tuns', hence the term 'tunnage', which referred originally to the number of tuns a ship could carry.

There was some contact with the Mediterranean, and that brought exotic products to British shores from even further afield. Venetian fleets arrived at Southampton and Sandwich. They included large ships known as carracks, bearing goods that were rarely seen. In 1383 one at Sandwich was described as 'of astonishing size, full of treasures [such as] fruit, spices of various kinds, oil and so forth'.

The Development of the Ship

The development of the ship was slow and incremental, and there was no dominant outside influence comparable with the Romans and the Vikings in past ages. Ships were still single-masted, with one square sail. The main type was the keel, a descendant of the Viking ships with curved ends, a deep keel, and clinker build with overlapping planks. Another

The Port of Southampton

LEFT
The Norman Bargate at Southampton, the main land entrance to the medieval town and port.

THE Southampton area was settled by the Romans, but its rise as a major port began at the end of the twelfth century. It was well situated where the Itchen and Test rivers flow into Southampton Water, which had a double tide to help carry ships up and down it. The prevailing wind was at right angles to it so that ships could get in and out easily. The port had sea routes to Flanders and northern France for the export of wool and the import of wine. It also had routes by river and cartage to the important towns of Winchester and Salisbury, and further afield to London, Oxford and Leicester.

The medieval borough was roughly quadrilateral in shape, with the shore forming two sides and the city walls the others. It had a population of about 2500. Ships loaded and unloaded at the West Quay and the Town Quay to the south. Entrance from the north was via the Bargate, which still survives. There was a castle to the north-west within the walls.

The walls were strong on the landward side, but defences to seaward conflicted with the business of loading and unloading ships. In October 1338 the French raided the town with great destruction and looting. A decade later, Southampton was one of the ports through which the Black Death entered England, and the population fell by perhaps 40 per cent.

Southampton revived as a great port in the late nineteenth century, replacing Liverpool as a terminus for the great Atlantic liners. Despite bombing in the Second World War and post-war rebuilding, the line of the medieval walls can largely be seen today, and the Medieval Wool House has become a maritime museum.

type, more Mediterranean in origin, was the hulc, which had a different arrangement of planks towards the bow and stern. The cog came from the Frisian islands off Germany and Holland and had straight stem and stern posts. Over the years ships increased slightly in size and in the sophistication of their rigging. Castles were built in the bow and stern and became more permanent over the years, but still on a hull that would have been recognisable to the Vikings.

There were two developments that changed the nature of seafaring. The first was the compass, developed by the Chinese and adopted by the Arabs in the Mediterranean. It was noticed by Europeans by the time of the Third Crusade and was soon used by the English. It allowed a ship to steer a steady course when out of sight of land and when the sky was obscured and was particularly useful in northern waters.

The second was the stern rudder. Until the twelfth century, ships had been steered by an oar hung over the side near the stern. It was pivoted about its centre, so that the effort needed to turn it was minimised. A short tiller projected inboard for the use of the helmsman. From the twelfth century, shipbuilders began to hang the rudder on hinges on the sternpost. It now turned on one edge and needed more effort to operate it, but the tiller could be made much longer and eventually it was attached to other devices such as the whipstaff and the steering wheel. The stern rudder cleared the way for the building of much larger ships. It also had a profound effect on design. If it was to be hinged on more than two places, it needed a straight stern post. Also, it needed a clear 'run' so that the water came easily to it, to make it effective. Ships could no longer be double-ended as they had been in Viking times.

Henry V's *Grace Dieu* showed the limits of clinker construction in the Viking tradition. To build a vessel of such size it was necessary to use a triple skin construction, which was clumsy and difficult. English shipbuilders were beginning to look to the Mediterranean where a different type of construction was common. In carvel building, the frame of the ship was of far greater importance in producing its shape, and the planks were laid edge to edge with no overlap. This allowed much bigger ships, and the way was open for expansion. The three-masted ship originated in the Mediterranean and in Spain and Portugal, and soon spread to Britain, and allowed a great expansion of seaborne trade, warfare, exploration, colonisation and emigration.

BELOW
A two-masted ship from around 1415 on the end of a bench in St Nicholas's Chapel in King's Lynn, Norfolk.

Chapter 4
Sea Power Under Sail

Henry VIII and the Birth of the Warship

Guns were often carried on warships in the late Middle Ages as a supplement to arrows and spears. The true birth of the warship, however, came when heavy guns were fitted low down in the ship, firing though gunports, which could be closed in rough weather. Two royal cousins, James IV of Scotland and Henry VIII of England, had a hand in this. For the only time in Scottish history, James IV tried to build a strong navy, including the *Great Michael* of 1000 tons, one of the first ships to rely on heavy guns for the main armament. She out-classed Henry's largest ship, the *Mary Rose*, and the English King replied with the *Henri Grâce à Dieu*, more popularly known as the *Great Harry*.

Soon Henry would find both the means and the motive to build a great navy. He isolated himself from the great European powers in 1531 when he made himself head of the Church of England and looted the rich monasteries to finance his wars. From this point Protestantism would provide a motive for rebellion and war against the English state. It would cause the English and later the British to feel separate from Europe (even though the north Germans, Scandinavians and Dutch were equally Protestant) and increase their paranoia about foreign invasion. All this would make a strong navy more necessary.

Henry's sea power was tested during a war with France and Scotland (not yet Protestant) in 1544–6. It was not entirely successful – the *Mary Rose* was lost off Portsmouth while manoeuvring into battle against the French. An engagement in the Channel between eight English and eight French ships the following year proved indecisive. Henry was succeeded by his son Edward VI then by his eldest daughter Mary. Her unpopularity as a Catholic was compounded when she lost the last European possession, Calais, to the French. But it was a step in the evolution of the island nations, which now had no permanent continental commitments and were beginning to look further overseas.

Elizabeth and the Armada

Mary was succeeded by her half-sister Elizabeth, a staunch but moderate Protestant. She had no great wish for war with Spain, but English seamen such as Francis Drake were raiding the Spanish empire with her connivance, and she was giving support to Dutch Protestant rebels against Spanish rule in the Netherlands. These acts, coupled with his zeal to eliminate heresy, caused Philip II, King of Spain and ruler of much of Europe and Latin America, to send out his 'Invincible Armada' of 130 ships and nearly 30,000 men. He planned to sail them up the English Channel

to link up with the Spanish army in the Netherlands, then take the troops across to invade England.

Despite her frugality, Elizabeth had been building up a strong navy. John Hawkins had a key role in developing new ships, which put gun power and seaworthiness ahead of grandeur. Matthew Baker, one of the Queen's shipwrights, not only designed some of the 'race-built' galleons, but recorded them in a manuscript. Converted merchant ships were also used, and Elizabeth's forces included 34 warships and 163 merchantmen, mostly very small. The country was in a state of high alert when the Armada was sighted off Plymouth in July 1588. Beacons were set up on the hillsides ready to be lit if the enemy landed.

Although Elizabeth's ships were committed to gun power, this did not mean that they used broadsides as in a later sense. Instead, Tudor ships were designed for all-round fire, with the main armament firing ahead – Sir Walter Raleigh claimed that 'a ship of war doth pretend to fight most with his prow'. A ship would edge up on an opponent, fire her bow and one broadside, then tack to fire the other broadside and discharge her stern guns before retreating to reload.

The English fleet pursued the Spanish Armada for a week up the Channel and did little real damage. In the end it was the English fireships, the impracticability of the task they had set themselves, and storms that wrecked Philip's great expedition. Spain's days as a great power were numbered, the English gained confidence as a sea power that would never really leave them, and they later transmitted it to the other peoples of the United Kingdom.

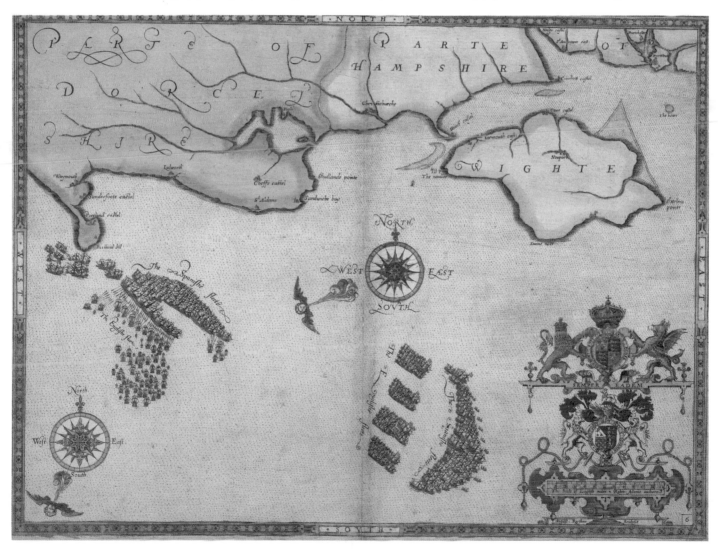

Mary Rose

THE *Mary Rose*, named after King Henry VIII's favourite sister, was built at Portsmouth in 1510. She was one of the first ships to deploy an armament of heavy guns mounted low on her decks and firing through gunports – although she also had high castles and carried many light guns and even longbows.

She sailed as flagship of Sir Edward Howard's fleet in 1511, in an expedition against Cadiz. She was in action for the first time the following year, when Howard successfully attacked the French at Brest. In 1513 she helped carry an English army to Calais and then supported a campaign against Scotland.

After being refitted in 1536, the *Mary Rose* carried an armament of 15 heavy brass guns, 54 lighter, breech-loading wrought iron guns and 70 light hailshot and hand guns to be fired from the tops and the bow and stern castles. Some fired forward and some into the waist between the castles. Her crew included 200 sailors, 185 soldiers and 30 gunners who operated the heavier weapons. In Anthony Anthony's Roll of Henry VIII's navy of 1546, she is listed as 700 tons, second only to the *Henri Grâce à Dieu*.

But the *Mary Rose* had already been lost by that time. On 20 July 1545 she was part of the fleet in the Solent opposing a French force of 225 ships and 30,000 soldiers. The forces engaged off St Helens and the *Mary Rose* capsized while turning, perhaps because her gunports were left open. Despite this loss, the battle was inconclusive and the French withdrew.

In 1836 the wreck was investigated by the Deane brothers, pioneers of diving. In 1970 it was rediscovered by Alexander McKee and the remaining section of the hull was raised by a team led by Margaret Rule in 1982. About a third of the hull was raised, forming a cross section cut diagonally, showing four decks. It is on display in Portsmouth Historic Dockyard. Just as important is the collection of artefacts, including guns, bows, rigging, living utensils, surgeon's tools, clothes and examples of almost everything needed to live and work on board ship. Archaeologists continue to investigate the bow section of the ship.

ABOVE
A representation of the *Mary Rose* as she would have looked at sea, with a small number of sails set for running before the wind.

LEFT
The hull of the *Mary Rose* in dry dock at Portsmouth, showing a cross section of the ship and her decks.

The Early Stuart Navy

When James VI of Scotland succeeded to the English throne as James I on the death of Elizabeth in 1603, it was an important step towards political unity in Britain. Scotland still had her own Parliament, but now her foreign policy was linked to that of England. Scottish revolts were common for the next 140 years, but the Union of the Crowns gave the navy more prominence as the main defender of the realm. In the short term, however, it fell into decline, after James made peace with Spain in 1604.

The early Stuart monarchy was financially weak and often at odds with the classes represented in the English Parliament. The monarchy's most expensive duty was to provide a navy to defend the country and protect trade, but it had great difficulty in doing this. Parliament could raise taxes for it, but that would involve compromise by the king.

James built a great prestige ship, the *Royal Prince* of 1200 tons and 55 guns in 1610, and his son, Charles I, built a fleet of ships of around 40 guns as well as the largest ship of the day, the 100-gun *Sovereign of the Seas*. There was a growing recognition that the navy needed two main types of ship: large ones to defend the country against foreign navies – 'A Royal fleet destinated to meet with another of the like', and small fast ones to protect trade, such as the 14 'whelps' built by Charles. But expeditions to Cadiz and La Rochelle ended in disaster, and pirates from North Africa raided the British and Irish coasts. Charles tried to extend the ancient tax of Ship Money to inland towns and this contributed to the outbreak of Civil War between King and Parliament in 1642.

The Civil War

The navy supported Parliament, because it had been unpaid and underfed by the King. The war was mainly fought on land but sea power was important in preventing an intervention by European powers. As C V Wedgwood describes in *The King's War*: 'What mattered to the European nations was not so much who controlled the land, but who controlled the sea around England', and 'owing to Parliament's control of the sea no foreign power seriously contemplated armed intervention in the English fighting'. Parliament also needed small ships to deal with Royalist gun runners, and it copied the fast frigates of the Dunkirk privateers.

Charles was executed in 1649 and a republic was set up, but still it found no security. The Royalists continued to operate privateers, Scotland and Ireland were conquered, and there were naval wars with France and Spain. There was a great increase in the fleet, especially during the rule of Oliver Cromwell from 1653 to 1658, and a return to larger ships to fight enemy navies.

The Dutch Wars

The Anglo-Dutch wars were caused by the competition between the two nations for trade and colonies. When the first began in 1652 both nations were Protestant republics and should have been natural allies, but the Dutch resented the English attempt to exclude them from their trade by the Navigation Act of 1651. The wars were a formative experience for the English navy. Fought mainly in the southern part of the North Sea, they involved an average of about three battles per year, as the seafaring Dutch had no inclination to avoid combat and had to defeat the English strategy of destroying their trade by blockade. Huge fleets of up to 100 ships on each side were involved. The tactics of the early fights are unclear, but at the Battle of the Gabbard in 1653, George Monck put his whole fleet in a single line, so that the ships would not mask one another's gunfire. It was the beginning of the line

Chatham Dockyard

LEFT
Chatham Dockyard, as painted by Joseph Farington in the 1790s. The anchor wharf storehouses and the ropery are on the right, the building slips and dry docks are on the left, and the mast houses and other buildings are behind them.

THE Royal Dockyards were essential to the maintenance of the fleet under both sail and steam. They built ships for the navy, repaired them in dry docks, which gave them their name, produced a wide variety of fittings such as anchors and rope, and stored them ready for use. The River Medway provided an ideal site and Edward VI first set up a storehouse there in 1547. The first dry dock was built in 1625.

During the Dutch Wars between 1652 and 1674 Chatham was the most important naval base in the country as the only large one facing the North Sea. The Dutch raid on the Medway in 1667 stopped short of the dockyard itself, but some of the ships in its charge were captured or damaged. It was less in the front line during the French wars between 1689 and 1815, and concentrated more on shipbuilding and repair. HMS *Victory*, launched in 1765, was the most famous ship built there. The Dockyard was largely rebuilt in the course of the eighteenth century and surviving buildings include the Commissioners House (1704), Officers Terrace (1722–33), Sail loft (1723), Mast House and Mould Loft (1753–8) and the Ropery of 1786–91. The gatehouse of 1720 is a notable landmark of the area.

Early in the nineteenth century several covered slips were built to allow shipbuilding in shelter. Some were destroyed in a fire of 1966 but the remaining ones show the transition from wood to iron construction. The Dockyard was greatly expanded in 1865–85 by the building of three huge wet docks between the mainland and St Mary's Island north of the old site. The last battleship built at Chatham was the *Africa* of 1905, for the new Dreadnoughts were too large to negotiate the Medway. Instead the Dockyard found a new role in building and servicing submarines, down to the nuclear age when a servicing facility was built in 1970. Chatham Dockyard largely escaped bombing in the Second World War, unlike Portsmouth and Plymouth. When the Royal Navy left in 1984 the older part, consisting of 80 acres, became the first Historic Dockyard. It contains 47 historic listed buildings.

of battle, which would dominate naval tactics for nearly three centuries. The Dutch attacked piece-meal and were defeated. After another English victory, the Dutch made peace in 1654.

The consequence of this was that the 'ship of the line' became the main arbiter of naval power. It was arguably the first new ship type ever to originate in Britain. Unlike earlier ships it was not designed to turn in battle, but to stand and fight. It had to be a certain minimum size to meet a large enemy ship opposite it in the line. This varied over the years, from 50 guns in 1700 to 74 guns in 1815. At times, other nations such as the French would build more ships of the line than Britain, and some-times they would build better ones, but the ship of the line remained the basis of British sea power until it was replaced by steam nearly two centuries later.

The Second Dutch War began in 1665, five years after the restoration of the monarchy in Charles II. There were early English victories and the heroism of the seamen on both sides became legendary. Although Parliament had been enthusiastic at the start of the war, it failed to provide enough money to pursue it properly. In 1667 the English demanded stiff peace terms but did not send the fleet to sea. The Dutch replied with a daring raid on the naval base in the River Medway, capturing the English flag-ship *Royal Charles*. The blow to English morale was greater than the material damage, and peace was made soon afterwards.

The third war was opportunist as far as the English were concerned. This time they were allied with the French, who invaded the Netherlands by land and provided a naval squadron to support the English. The French squadron failed to help when the com-bined fleets were surprised by the Dutch. After that the Dutch kept behind the sandbanks on their own coast. The English and French attacked three times without success. Charles,

lacking money and popular support, was forced to make peace in 1674, although the French campaign continued on land.

Despite its failures in battle, Charles II's navy made much progress in ship design and naval administration, partly under the leadership of Samuel Pepys, who became Secretary of the Admiralty in 1673. He supervised the building of new ships while the shipwrights, such as his friend Sir Anthony Deane and his rivals of the Pett family, made many improvements in design. According to Pepys himself, nautical skills had been advanced under Charles 'per-haps beyond any improvement'.

Wars for Europe

Charles's brother became King as James II and supported Pepys in rescuing the navy from neg-lect, but his Roman Catholic policies made him unpopular and he was overthrown by the Dutchman, William of Orange in 1688. This began the first of a long series of wars with France, now the world's leading power under Louis XIV. The English and Dutch were defeat-ed at Beachy Head in 1690, but had their revenge at Barfleur and La Hogue two years later. After that the French abandoned their battle fleet strategy for nearly 40 years, and used small fast privateers to raid the expanding British commerce. This was not likely to win the war but it forced the Royal Navy to adopt new tactics and build smaller ships.

There was peace from 1697 to 1702, but Louis was still expanding his power. The War of Spanish Succession saw no great sea battles but the British captured Gibraltar and Minorca as naval bases, and gained trading rights with Spanish America. When peace was restored in 1714 the Royal Navy was unchallenged on the world's seas, and quickly sank into complacency. The 'establishments of dimensions' laid down sizes of every part of a ship and prevented progress. Old ships were 'rebuilt' keeping many of their old defects. Unsuccessful classes, such as the three-deckers of 80 guns, which had originated in the 1690s but had proved to have too many guns for a ship of their size and were unstable, were retained in service despite obvious faults. Tactically the line of battle reigned supreme and any admiral or captain who deviated from it was likely to face punishment.

Colonial Wars

In 1739, a certain Captain Jenkins produced an ear before the House of Commons claiming it had been cut off by a Spanish officer and war was declared on Spain. The public expected rich pickings and Admiral Vernon's expedition to capture Portobello was an early success. But other amphibious operations were soon bogged down and ravaged by disease, while Spanish warships, such as the 70-gun *Princessa*, proved surprisingly good in action. In 1740 Commodore Anson sailed round the world with a small squadron, harassing Spanish trade and colonies in the Pacific. He lost most of his men and all but one of his ships, but returned in 1744 as a rich man and a national hero. He became a Lord of the Admiralty and began to reform the navy, eventually building new ships, changing the promotion system of the officer corps and creating the marines in their modern form.

During his time away the conflict expanded and war broke out between Britain and France. Prince Charles, 'Bonnie Prince Charlie', the grandson of James II, landed in Scotland by sea to begin the 1745 rebellion, but French maritime support was at first reluctant, and then it was largely stopped by the Royal Navy's blockade, so the rebellion was defeated. Meanwhile Anson instituted a strong Western Squadron off the main French Atlantic base at Brest, and personally led a force that captured several French warships and East Indiamen off Cape Finisterre in 1747. The French were victorious in Europe and the British at sea, so a compromise peace was agreed in 1748.

As the sides shaped up for a new war that began in 1756, Anson ordered new ships for the navy. They were to carry 74 guns, as the latest French ones did, but they did not copy French design slavishly. They were the most effective ships of the line of the age, the ideal compromise between seaworthiness, gun power and performance. Anson also ordered many single-decker frigates based on French ideas, and the three-decker, 100-gun *Victory*, although she was not ready until the war was over and Anson was dead.

The war began badly for the British. Minorca was lost to the French and Admiral John Byng was court-martialled and shot as a scapegoat. But 1759 became the 'year of victories', in which Quebec, and therefore Canada, was taken from the French, and the main Brest fleet was driven into Quiberon Bay by Admiral Hawke and destroyed. North America and India were safely under British control and the British Empire seemed to reach a peak when the Seven Years War ended in 1763.

But Britain had abandoned her European allies and George III attempted to tax the American colonists, sparking off a revolt. As it grew into a national independence movement, the Royal Navy had much to do in support of the army. It moved its main base from Boston to New York in 1776 and helped organise and protect a huge fleet of transports which was needed to take troops and stores across to the continent. It landed troops to capture Philadelphia and Saratoga.

In 1778 the navy had a new role when France, seeking revenge for the loss of her colonies, entered the War of American Independence and was followed by Spain the following year. There were indecisive battles on

HMS *Victory*

RIGHT
The site in the cockpit of the *Victory* where Nelson is said to have died, although the exact location remains controversial.

IN December 1758, as the Seven Years War approached its climax, the Admiralty ordered a new first rate ship of 100 guns to be built in Chatham Dockyard. She was to have three complete decks of guns, plus more on the quarterdeck and forecastle. The largest ship yet built for the Royal Navy, she was designed by Thomas Slade and named *Victory*, but the war ended and she was not completed until 1765. She saw very little service in peacetime and did not go to sea until 1778, when she was needed to fight the French during the War of American Independence. The *Victory* was 186 feet long on the gundeck with 32 sails on three masts and a crew of about 850, who slept in hammocks on the lower and middle decks and ate from mess tables slung between the guns.

She was often used as an admiral's flagship and led the fleet into the indecisive battle off Ushant in Brittany in 1778. She was laid up 'in ordinary' after the war ended in 1783, with only a small team of shipkeepers to look after her. After the war with the French Revolutionaries broke out in 1793, she became the main flagship of the Mediterranean Fleet. She was Sir John Jervis's flagship when the Spanish were defeated off Cape St Vincent in 1797. Despite extensive repairs in 1788 she was beginning to show her age and was sent

The site in the cockpit of the *Victory* where Nelson is said to have died, although the exact location remains controversial.

home to become a hospital ship for French and Spanish prisoners in the Medway.

Her design was rather dated by this time and much larger first rates had been built, but her good sailing qualities made her a favourite with admirals. In 1800 she was taken into Chatham Dockyard for a 'large repair' which, in the end, would cost more than her original building. Many of her elaborate decorations were removed, but her basic hull shape was not changed. She was ready by the spring of 1803, just in time for Vice-Admiral Lord Nelson to hoist his flag in her in command of the Mediterranean Fleet. For the next two years she blockaded Toulon, until the French broke out and lured Nelson across the Atlantic. She took Nelson home briefly in 1805, then out to Cadiz where he led his division into the Battle of Trafalgar on 21 October. Her 132 dead and wounded included Nelson, who was shot on her quarterdeck and died below in her cockpit.

This did not end her active service and she was repaired and sent to the Baltic as Admiral Saumarez's flagship from 1809–12. She remained as a static guardship at Portsmouth and from the 1820s there was increasing public pressure to preserve her. She was retained afloat as a depot ship until 1903, when she was accidentally hit by a modern battleship. The Society for Nautical Research campaigned to have her put in a dry dock for preservation and this was achieved in 1922. She has gradually been restored to her condition as she entered the Battle of Trafalgar.

BELOW
The *Victory* at Portsmouth, showing the beakhead with a replica of the figurehead installed in 1803, and the masts and bowsprit towering above it.

both sides of the Atlantic, and the French and Spanish failed to press home their advantage and invade Britain. In 1782 the British General Cornwallis was isolated with his army at Yorktown in Virginia and the British fleet failed to rescue him. He had to surrender and the rebel position was greatly improved.

There was some technological innovation during the period. A new gun called the carronade had heavy fire power over a short range and gave some advantages. The navy had experimented with metal sheathing of ships' bottoms for many years to prevent weed and worm. By 1780 it had found a practical way to cover them in copper. It was expensive but very useful and gave the navy some advantage in a long war.

Colonial war continued between Britain and France, with several battles between small squadrons in Indian waters. The Spanish recaptured Minorca but failed to take Gibraltar. The main British and French fleets went to the West Indies in the 1780s to contest the extremely valuable colonies there. Off the Saintes near the French island of Martinique in April 1782, Admiral Rodney defeated a French force and captured several ships including the flagship. The British had to concede American independence and the United States was founded. But the rest of the British Empire, in the Caribbean and India, was saved.

Rodney's victory represented a new stage in tactical evolution. Since Anson's day the line of battle had become less sacred, but Rodney went

further in breaking through the enemy line in pursuit of victory. Within 20 years a new generation of admirals, led by Nelson, would adopt even more radical tactics.

At home, the Royal Dockyards at Portsmouth and Plymouth and on the rivers Thames and Medway had developed into giant industrial organisations. Dozens of private shipyards also built ships for the navy, mostly sited near the Royal Dockyards where they could be supervised. The largest of these was at Blackwall on the Thames, which could build seven or eight ships simultaneously. The best known of the smaller ones was at Buckler's Hard in Hampshire, a tiny village which nevertheless built ships of the line and frigates. By the end of the War of American Independence the

Royal Navy had more than 600 ships. Twenty years later it had nearly a thousand.

Revolutionary Wars

Britain declared war on the French Revolutionaries in 1793, a year after Louis XVI and Marie Antoinette had been guillotined. With the alliance of all the other European powers and the French navy in a state of disorganisation, an easy victory seemed likely until the French armies rallied and drove their enemies back. The British had one naval success on the 'Glorious First of June' in 1794, when Admiral Howe's fleet captured six French ships of the line and sank one.

The British occupied the great French Mediterranean port of Toulon for a time in

1794, but failed to burn enough enemy ships as a young artillery major, Napoleon Bonaparte, forced them to withdraw. Two years later, as Spain entered the war against Britain, the Royal Navy had to abandon the Mediterranean. In 1797 the fleet mutinied at Spithead and the Nore but it won victories against the Spanish at Cape St Vincent and the Dutch at Camperdown. The new rising star, Horatio Nelson, played a key role at St Vincent but lost an arm at Tenerife a few months later.

Early in 1798 the British Government received reports that the French were preparing a great fleet of warships and transports with troops for an unknown destination. Admiral Nelson was sent to look for them and after many vicissitudes he found them anchored in Aboukir Bay, Egypt, where they had landed an army. He attacked at once, despite the failing light, and Captain Foley of the 74-gun *Goliath* led part of the fleet round to the enemy's blind side in a devastating move. It was Nelson's idea of a battle of annihilation in which 12 out of 14 enemy ships of the line were captured or destroyed.

Apart from the great battle fleets, British frigates and sloops were conducting a different kind of war. They escorted convoys numbering up to 1000 ships, chased privateers, and carried out numerous duties of war. It was in single-ship actions against enemy frigates that the British demonstrated their superiority, brought about mainly by the better training and seafaring experience of their crews. A British frigate was likely to triumph against a French ship of 50 per cent larger crew and gun power. The most dramatic action of all came in 1800 when Lord Cochrane, in command of the sloop *Speedy,* captured *El Gamo,* a Spanish frigate four times her size.

In 1801 Nelson was sent under the command of Admiral Sir Hyde Parker to deal with the Danish fleet at Copenhagen. He led his ships towards an enemy line drawn up in front of the city and fought a very fierce battle. When the Danish Crown Prince offered a truce

BELOW
The quarterdeck of the *Victory* during the height of the Battle of Trafalgar, painted by Denis Dighton, with the wounded Nelson on the right. Gun crews are seen in action on the left, with marines firing muskets to the left and right.

he accepted it, but claimed victory. Meanwhile in Egypt, Admiral Lord Keith landed an army which defeated the remnants of Bonaparte's French force. But unknown to the British on the spot, the war was about to end. Not for the first time, the British were victorious on sea and the French on land, and peace was signed at Amiens in 1801.

When war resumed in 1803, the British feared an invasion by the large fleet of barges Bonaparte (soon to become Emperor Napoleon) was assembling at Boulogne. Nelson was put in charge of the Mediterranean Fleet to blockade the French at Toulon. In 1805 the French evaded him and led him across the Atlantic to the West Indies, where they planned to double back and give the French superiority in the English Channel. Nelson saw through the ruse and got the news back by fast frigate. A scratch force was assembled under Admiral Calder off Cape Finisterre and forced the French into the Spanish port of Ferrol. They moved to Cadiz and joined more Spanish ships, to create a huge and threatening force of more than 30 ships of the line. Nelson, after three weeks on shore, was sent to blockade them.

Goaded by Napoleon, the French Admiral Villeneuve led his Franco-Spanish fleet of 33 ships out of harbour. He was met by Nelson's 27 of the line on 21 October off Cape Trafalgar. Nelson had planned to attack with three groups of ships, but had less available than expected, so Admiral Collingwood led one division into battle at right angles to the French, and Nelson led the other. It developed into a mêlée battle in which Nelson was fatally wounded. Eighteen of the enemy fleet were captured, but the majority were lost in a storm that followed the battle.

It was a great victory, but it did not end the war. British forces controlled the Mediterranean, escorted convoys and blockaded the numerous small ports which were refusing to trade with Britain as a result of Napoleon's Continental System. The navy aided a Spanish and Portuguese revolt against Napoleon from 1808, and supported the armies of the Duke of Wellington as they fought the Peninsular War. Napoleon was distracted by his disastrous invasion of Russia in 1812, and Wellington crossed the Pyrenees while the Russians and their allies invaded France from another direction. The Emperor was forced to abdicate and go into exile.

In 1812 another war broke out between Britain and the USA over the British practice of inspecting American ships. The British blockaded the US coast and raided it, burning the President's residence so that it had to be repainted and given the name of White House. The Americans retaliated with their very effective frigates, which shocked the British in a series of single-ship engagements, as when the USS *Constitution* captured HMS *Guerriere*. The British finally had a success when HMS *Shannon* captured the *Chesapeake* off Boston in 1813. The war ended in 1815.

Napoleon escaped from his exile on Elba and reclaimed the throne of France. He was defeated at Waterloo in Belgium in 1815 and fled, eventually surrendering to HMS *Bellerophon* of 74 guns. He was taken to a stricter exile on the remote island of St Helena. The great age of European war was over. The French were exhausted by years of bloodshed and their navy was defeated, leaving Britain as the only real sea power for the moment.

The Last Campaigns

Britain would not be involved in another major war for nearly a century after 1815, and the navy was rapidly reduced, but still found work to do. In 1816 it combined with the Dutch to attack Algiers, a centre for corsairs who took European shipping and slaves. It mounted patrols to try to eliminate the slave trade off the coast of West Africa. The last sailing-ship battle was fought in 1827, when the French and British fleets eliminated a Turkish squadron at Navarino off the coast of Greece, which was fighting for its independence from Turkey. Steam was already in use on the fringes of the fleet, and Lord Cochrane, dismissed from the Royal Navy and in charge of the Greek navy, used it on behalf of the Greeks. Steam would come to dominate the seas, although that did not stop the continued rise of British sea power.

Chapter 5
Trade under Sail

The three-masted sailing ship had evolved in the Mediterranean and Iberia around the middle of the fifteenth century and by 1500 it was common in British waters. It combined the best of the Mediterranean and Viking traditions, with square sails from the latter. From the Mediterranean it took the triangular lateen sail on its third mast, the mizzen, and clinker building in which the frame was constructed first and the planks were added, flush with one another to present a smooth surface. As well as increasing the sail area available to an individual ship, the three-mast arrangement allowed a more balanced rig, in which some sails could be backed to give leverage when tacking through the wind. It led to a further increase of the sail area over the years, with new sails being added above the lower ones – the topsails – then the topgallants, then the royals. This allowed smaller sails, which were easier to handle. The carvel building system, combined with the use of plans from the late sixteenth century, allowed the development of much bigger ships.

The Hansa League, which had dominated the trade of northern Europe since the thirteenth century, was in decline and the Dutch were rising as the most important merchants and shipowners of the region, with a strong trade to the Baltic and elsewhere. In 1560, at the beginning of Elizabeth I's long reign, the English merchant fleet had only 50,000 tons of shipping. This soon began to rise, partly through fishing

and partly because of a great growth in the coal trade from Newcastle, which increased from 35,000 tons in 1550, to 140,000 at the end of the century. The Dutch were fighting for their independence from Spain and their huge merchant fleet was hampered. By 1629 the English had over 115,000 tons of shipping. More than 145 of these ships were of 200 tons or more. They were built as 'defensible ships', with a strong armament to beat off attack, unlike Dutch ships which were designed to carry the maximum goods with the minimum crew.

The Navigation Acts

In 1651 the English Parliament passed the Navigation Acts. These decreed that English trade could only be carried in English ships, built in England or taken as prizes in war, and with largely English crews. Foreign trade with parts of the Empire was forbidden, and imports could only come in English ships, or those from the country of origin of the goods. It was intended to develop the use of English ships and the training of seamen, who might be taken into the navy in time of need, but was clearly a blow to the Dutch, who made their living in the very trades that were prohibited, and it led to the first of three wars between them and the English. The Acts were confirmed at the restoration of Charles II in 1660, and remained British policy for nearly two centuries.

One important effect of the Anglo-Dutch

Wars was the capture of up to 3000 economical Dutch merchant ships, which became part of the English merchant service. They also showed English shipbuilders how to build cheap ships. The latter part of the seventeenth century saw a boom in the trades with America and the West Indies, and with northern Europe. Timber was in great demand for rebuilding London after the great fire of 1666, and for both merchant and naval shipbuilding. Large quantities were imported from the Baltic.

The Canal Age

Canals had been in use on a small scale for many years. The Exeter Canal was built in 1566 after the River Exe was blocked by a weir. A new age began in 1760, when the Duke of Bridgewater constructed a canal to take coal from his mines at Worsley to the River Mersey. The great engineer, Thomas Telford, showed the advantages of canals when he calculated that a packhorse could carry an eighth of a ton of coal on its back. The same horse could draw 2 tons on a good road, 30 tons on a barge on a river, or 50 tons on a canal barge.

Most canals were built for specially designed barges known as narrow boats. They linked navigable rivers and opened up expanding industrial towns such as Birmingham and Manchester. In Scotland, the Crinan Canal

BELOW
Trading in slaves at Barbados. The picture illustrates a traditional tale in which a white Englishman sells his African lover into slavery. To the left is a typical merchant ship of the period. In the background on the right is a fort, while towards the centre a naval frigate is drying its sails.

Birmingham Canals

BIRMINGHAM seems an unlikely centre for maritime history. Unlike the great majority of British cities it has neither a port nor a navigable river. Its centre is on a plateau 145 metres above sea level and it is some way from the Rivers Avon, Trent and Severn. Its history and growth is inextricably linked with the canal age and its population rose from 30,000 in 1770 to nearly 250,000 in 1851. Its first canal was the Birmingham Canal, linking the growing town to the coalfields and Wolverhampton, which was partly operational by 1769 and fully opened in 1773. By 1830 the city was at the crossroads of the national network. It had the Worcester and Birmingham Canal (1791), which led to the Bristol Channel. The Trent and Mersey or Grand Trunk Canal (1766) took goods to the north-west, as did the Birmingham and Liverpool from 1826. There was a route to the Humber and north-east England through canals and the River Trent. The city had links to the Grand Junction Canal of 1791, which led to London and the River Thames. Only in the west did the canal link fail to materialise. Barges could once go along the Leominster Canal, but the Welsh mountains defeated any further movement in that direction.

Birmingham still has more miles of canal than Venice, penetrating into the city centre. Highlights include the Wast Hill tunnel, one of the longest in the country at 2491 metres; the unusual guillotine lock at the join of the Worcester and Birmingham and Stratford Canals; the Farmers Bridge flight of 13 locks; and the contrast where the Birmingham and Fazeley Canal passes under the motorway interchange, Spaghetti Junction.

across the Kintyre peninsula and the Caledonian Canal through the Great Glen were ship canals. By the time they were completed, in 1803 and 1822, they were too small for the increasingly large ships of the day.

By the 1830s, the canals were gradually supplanted by the railways as the main means of inland goods transport. Canal building largely ceased, except for the Manchester Ship Canal of 1893, which was intended to follow the success of Glasgow in creating its own route to its port, but it was never profitable. In the twentieth century inland waterways were gradually taken over for leisure use, although they continued to be important in some coal-mining areas, for example around the River Humber.

The Eighteenth Century

Throughout the eighteenth century, the interests of the great trading companies were balanced against those of small-scale merchants and shipowners. The East India Company became enormously powerful, far beyond their original trading aims, but it was smaller scale enterprise that did most of the business in North America and the West Indies.

The end of the War of Spanish Succession in 1714, and the possibility of trade with Spanish America, opened up another prospect of great riches. The South Sea Company was founded to take advantage of this. It was allowed to send an annual ship to sell goods at Vera Cruz in Mexico. In practice, it was alleged, it had tenders off shore, which ferried on more goods. The company also had the *asiento*, or contract, to sell slaves to Spanish America. In 1720 the company overreached itself by taking over the National Debt and crashed in the South Sea Bubble – an event that led to the abolition of joint-stock companies and made investors very

cautious for the next century or so. However, maritime law was different and offered a good outlet for small investors, for ships were usually divided into 16 or 32 shares.

English trade remained relatively stable for the first three-quarters of the eighteenth century, interrupted by numerous wars with France and Spain. Coal was now by far the greatest export by volume, which made it the largest user of shipping. Corn was exported from East Anglia in the first half of the century, but it was mainly needed to feed the growing urban populations in later years. Manufactures consisted mainly of woollen goods and hats. Newfoundland cod, caught and carried in British ships, fed much of the poor population of southern Europe.

The English and Scottish Parliaments were united in 1707, and the Scots were given a share in the Empire. The merchants of Glasgow used this to the full, sending ships to the North American colonies to import tobacco and then re-export much of it to Europe. The Clyde had the natural advantage that its ships were routed round the north of Ireland away from French privateers. The river was deepened to transform the rising city into an important port. The great merchants, the 'tobacco lords' mainly survived the effects of American independence in 1776, by switching to other trades such as cotton.

Historians are divided about whether industrial change in England and Scotland in the late nineteenth century amounted to a 'revolution' or not. In any case it had comparative little immediate effect on the technology of merchant shipping, but the expanding coal, textile and iron industries caused a great growth in merchant shipping. Cotton was imported from North America and the West Indies, coal was exported in large quantities from Ayrshire, Fife and north-east England. The growing iron industry included the Carron Iron Works near Falkirk in Scotland, which invented a new type of gun called the carronade and produced it in large quantities. New export markets were found for manufactures in Europe and the Empire.

A stable infrastructure and insurance market was essential to the development of merchant shipping. Lloyd's of London was founded as a coffee house in 1688, the shipping newspaper *Lloyd's List* first appeared in 1734, and the *Register of Ships* in the 1760s. The standard form of insurance policy was drawn up in 1779, and Lloyd's gained greatly in reputation during the Napoleonic Wars.

The Slave Trade

Hawkins and Drake were the first Englishmen to try to get into the trade in slaves between West Africa and America and the West Indies. In 1567 their ships were attacked by the Spanish at San Juan de Ullua in the Gulf of Mexico. In the seventeenth century the British acquired colonies of their own in North America and the West Indies, and soon began to import slaves to work the sugar and tobacco plantations. Between 1690 and 1807 it is estimated that British ships carried nearly 3 million slaves. Originally the ships were under charter to the Royal African Company, founded in 1670. The main ports were Liverpool, Bristol and London, although many smaller ports took a part. On the outward voyage the ships carried trade goods, such as iron bars, weapons and baubles. On arrival off the African coast, the ship's officers bargained for slaves with local agents or African slave-owners. Often it took months to fill a ship. Then they sailed for America, the notorious 'middle passage' of the 'triangular trade', when conditions were most horrific and many died. Having sold the slaves in the West Indies, the ship returned with a cargo of sugar. Not all ships trading with the West Indies used the triangular routes – many operated direct between British ports and the islands, taking out manufactured goods.

The slave trade did not disturb the European conscience until after 1750. Abolitionists, such as John Newton who had once been a slave ship captain himself, succeeded in having an act passed in 1807 to prohibit the taking of any new slave, although the existing slaves and their descendants continued in bondage for another 27 years. After 1815 the British prevailed on other nations to abolish the trade and used the Royal Navy to suppress it, with varying success.

RIGHT
Slaves crammed into the French ship *Vigilante*, captured by the Royal Navy off the coast of Africa in 1822. With the abolition of the trade in 1808, conditions became even worse in ships run by illegal traders.

The representation of the brig Vigilante from Nantes, a vessel employed in the Slave Trade, which was captured by Lieutenant Mildmay in the River Bonny, on the Coast of Africa, on the 15th of April 1822. She was 240 Tons burden & had on board at the time she was taken 345 Slaves. The Slaves were found lying on their backs on the lower deck, as represented below; those in the centre were sitting, some in the posture in which they are there shewn & others with their legs bent under them, resting upon the soles of their feet.

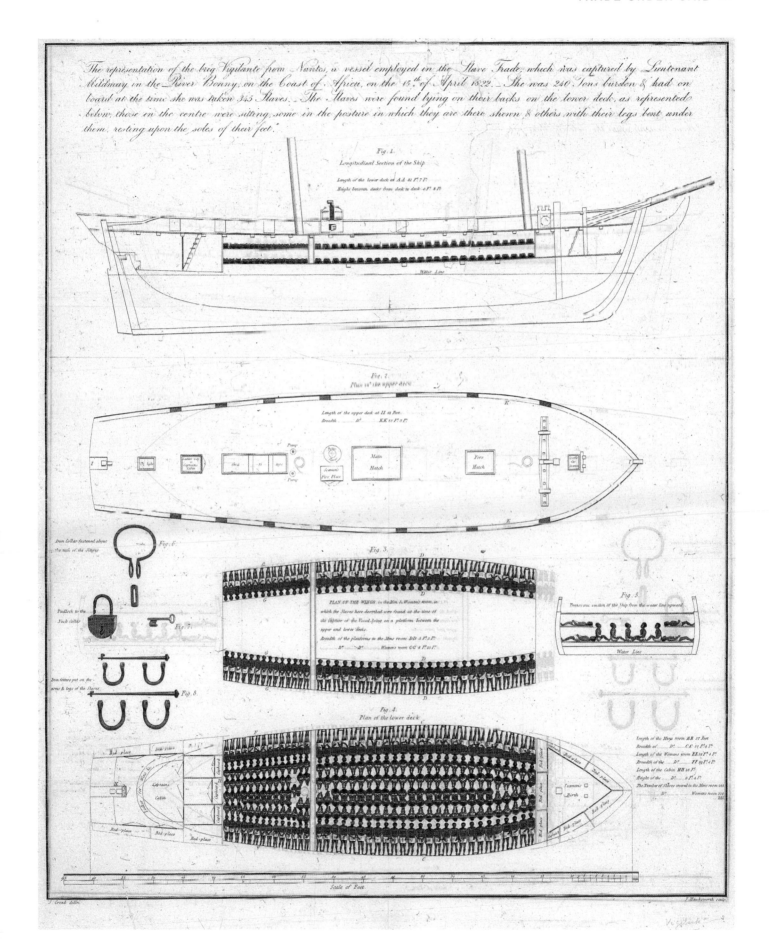

Fig. 1.
Longitudinal Section of the Ship

Fig. 2.
Plan of the upper deck

Fig. 3.

PLAN OF THE WINGS in the Men & Women's room, in which the Slaves here described were found at the time of the capture of the Vessel lying on a platform between the upper and lower decks.

Fig. 5.

Fig. 4.
Plan of the lower deck

Iron Collar fastened about the neck of the Slaves. Fig. 6.

Padlock to the Neck collar. Fig. 7.

Iron fetters put on the arms & legs of the Slaves. Fig. 8.

Scale of Feet.

Thames Barge *Centaur*

EVERY area of Britain evolved its own type of craft, suited to local conditions. Square rig was in use in certain areas such as the Humber Estuary and the River Teign in Devon. Most other boats used fore-and-aft rig in order to get closer to the wind in narrow spaces.

The Thames barge had Dutch features such as the leeboards, which were let down to prevent it being driven sideways in the wind, and the sprit rig, which kept the centre of gravity of the rigging as low as possible. The rather square, flat-bottomed hull was more English in its conception. In the course of the nineteenth century it tended to acquire labour-saving devices such as iron winches, so that it could be operated by a crew of three. Thames barges traded all round the estuary, up the coast to Harwich and beyond and along the north Kent coast. They could pick up agricultural cargoes from small ports such

as Pin Mill on the River Orwell, and they were often seen on the way to London looking like a floating haystack with the helmsman sitting on top. Often they returned with manure from London's horses. Other barges carried bricks or general cargoes. All had folding masts, which were lowered to pass under the Thames and Medway bridges. Some had a reduced rig to operate far up the Thames above London, where they were towed by horses if the wind was unsuitable. Thames barge races began in the 1840s and continue to the present day.

The *Centaur* was built in 1895 by Cann Brothers of Harwich for Charles Stone. At 85 feet long and of 61 gross tons, she was typical of many vessels of the time. In 1974, when her skipper Tom Baker retired, he sold her to the Thames Barge Sailing Trust, which operates her on charters from Maldon in Essex.

The Eighteenth-Century Sailing Ship

In the middle of the eighteenth century the Swedish naval architect Frederick Hendrik af Chapman studied in England and published a book on the naval architecture of merchant ships. He described several types, including the largest, 'frigate built', which had a full figurehead and a counter and galleries at the stern. The pink was based on the old Dutch freighter design, while cats and barks had no figurehead and very little of a gallery at the stern. Of smaller vessels, British types included the herring buss, the smack for flatfish, the cutter, and the un-powered lighter and single-masted hoy used for transport out to ships in the Thames Estuary.

Most ships were quite slow, but speed was not a great asset. In wartime a convoy went at the speed of the slowest ship so there was little motive to improve, except in 'privateers' or private men-of-war. Owners found it more economical to build ships to carry large cargoes, such as the almost-square Newcastle and Whitby colliers. Most ships of above 200 tons or so were square rigged, with three masts. Smaller ones were brigs, with two square-rigged masts. They often crossed the Atlantic, for example on the Glasgow tobacco trade. Fore-and-aft rigged vessels could sail closer to the wind, but long-distance trades tended to follow the wind in any case. Only the smallest vessels, for use in estuaries and cross-channel passages, were fore-and-aft rigged. They included local craft such as the Thames barge, the Humber keel and the Mersey flat, each adapted to the conditions in its area. Among the fastest were cutters, single-masted boats developed by smugglers to bring in goods from France, and soon copied by the navy.

Pirates and Smugglers

The British Isles were plagued by pirates at times when the Royal Navy was weak, especially during the reigns of James I and Charles I. There were many raids on the English coast by corsairs based in North Africa and in 1631 the village of Baltimore in Ireland was raided. More than 100 people, almost the whole population,

were taken into slavery. The corsairs were driven away from the British coasts by the development of a much stronger navy, but continued to raid shipping in the Mediterranean for many years afterwards.

Piracy had its 'golden age' in the Caribbean in the seventeenth and early eighteenth centuries, as competing state authorities and the aftermath of wars led to weak government control. Henry Morgan had his heyday in the 1660s and 1670s when he captured Portobello and Panama. There was another boom at the end of the first series of Anglo-French wars after 1714, when Edward Teach or 'Blackbeard' flourished until his death in 1718. It was largely under control by 1720, although low-level piracy continued until about 1830.

Behind the façade of great architecture and elegant life for the upper classes, the eighteenth century was a lawless age. Ships sailing into

BELOW
Captain Henry Morgan at the sack of Panama in 1671.

LEFT
A romantic view of the pirate captain William Kidd (hanged in 1701) burying his treasure, by the American illustrator Howard Pyle.

port were often pillaged for goods, and there was further thieving in the areas where they were unloaded. High customs duties on wine and brandy created a lucrative smuggling industry, especially on the south coast of England. Their trade was not seen as antisocial and smugglers became folk heroes in many parts of Cornwall and Devon. In Scotland the high duties after the Union of 1707 were seen as an English imposition and the hanging of a smuggler sparked off the Porteous riots of 1736, when the city of Edinburgh was under mob rule for several days.

The Perfection of the Sailing Ship

Early in the nineteenth century, the merchant sailing ship began to benefit from developments which had started in the Royal Navy – improved pumps, coppering of bottoms and the structural improvements introduced by naval architect Robert Seppings, for example. But a much greater revolution was on the way, partly inspired by the competition with steamships. The monopolies of the old chartered companies were abolished and for the first time in centuries, speed became an advantage in a merchant ship. The Gold Rushes to California and Australia created demand for even faster ships in the middle of the century. Technology also contributed. New methods of rope-making allowed much thinner cordage, which created less drag when sailing into the wind. Wire was used for the standing rigging that supported the masts. In a relatively peaceful world, ships no longer had to carry guns and that made the designer's task much easier. Steam also helped in a way, for ships could now be towed into port or up river, and did not have to be designed to make short tacks in restricted waters. Crews had to be reduced to compete with steam, so sails were subdivided to make them easier to handle.

All this led to the fast sleek clipper ship and the legendary tea races of the second half of the nineteenth century. The opening of the Suez Canal in 1869 made the route to India much easier for steamships and ended these races, but clipper ships then moved into the wool trade with Australia. Iron and steel shipbuilding allowed even larger vessels, often with more than three masts. For example, the *Wendur* of 1884 was of more than 2000 tons with four masts.

Inshore and closer to home, the coasting schooner mainly used a two-masted fore-and-aft rig with square topsails for running before the wind. Thousands of them were in use in the later nineteenth century. Local craft such as the Thames barge were perfected, often using the new iron construction and adopting labour saving devices such as winches to operate with a very small crew. Such trades flourished until the U-boat campaign of the First World War, after which road transport and increased restrictions put an end to them.

Cutty Sark

THE clipper ship *Cutty Sark* took her name from the fastest of the witches in Robert Burns's poem *Tam O'Shanter*. Captain John Willis ordered a ship of 1000 tons from Hercules Linton of Dumbarton in the hope that she would prove the fastest in the tea trade. She had very fine hull lines and was built with teak planks on an iron frame, but her high specification drove her builder into bankruptcy and she was completed by the neighbouring yard of Denny Brothers. She was ship rigged with three masts. Her topsails were divided vertically to make them easy to furl, for she never had a crew of more than 28 men. The officers lived in cabins and a saloon in the stern, with the crew and apprentices in deckhouses and in the forecastle, keeping the hold clear for cargo.

Entering service in 1869, she was doubly unlucky. The opening of the Suez Canal that year drove sailing ships out of the trade with India and she switched to carrying wool from Australia. And she never quite succeeded in beating her rival, the *Thermopylae* of Aberdeen. Their closest race came in 1872 when both sailed from Shanghai on the same tide. The *Cutty Sark* was 400 miles ahead when she lost her rudder. It took time to fit a temporary one and she lost the race but captured the public imagination. In 1878 her first mate killed one of the crew and was eventually jailed for manslaughter. Her fastest run from Australia to Britain was 69 days.

In 1895 she was sold to Ferreira of Portugal and her rig was reduced to a barquentine. In 1922 she was bought by Captain William Dowman, who converted her to a training ship at Falmouth. She transferred to the Thames and in 1954 she was opened to the public in a specially constructed dry dock at Greenwich. The ship was awarded a £12.95 million grant by the Heritage Lottery Fund in January 2005 to aid its conservation.

Chapter 6
Exploration and Empire

The English in America

The English were not far behind the Spanish and the Portuguese in the European discovery of the rest of the world. Columbus had already crossed the Atlantic (though he did not know he had discovered America) and Vasco da Gama was in the process of finding the sea route to India, when an 85-ton ship sailed from the port of Bristol in 1497. She was captained by John Cabot, an Italian who had been commissioned by Henry VII to seek new lands to the west. It is not quite certain where he eventually landed but he gave it the name Newfoundland and it became attached to an island off the North American coast. It was the true beginning of British interest in the 'New World' across the Atlantic, although it would be more than a century before regular colonisation began.

Francis Drake was a privateer captain who reconciled his Protestant religion with his predatory instincts by attacking Roman Catholic Spain, her ships and her colonies. He raided Panama in 1572 and became a popular hero. In 1577 he set out with the *Golden Hind* and four other ships, sailed through the Strait of Magellan and headed north, landing in California and Vancouver. He sailed across the Pacific and returned home in 1580, the first Briton to sail round the world. He was now fabulously wealthy and was knighted by Queen Elizabeth. He had opened up his countrymen's eyes to the possibilities of world trade and exploration.

ABOVE
Terracotta bust of Sir Walter Raleigh by John Michael Rysbrack.

There were several attempts to found English colonies in America during Elizabeth's reign. One of the best known was in 1584 when Walter Raleigh led a party to the island of Roanoke, off the coast of present-day North Carolina, part of a region known to the English as Virginia after

Elizabeth the 'virgin queen'. Raleigh himself became involved in the war against the Spanish Armada. Contact was lost with the settlers, who may have survived for many years but disappeared from history.

The First North American Colonies
In April 1607 three ships – the *Susan Constant, Godspeed* and *Discovery* – arrived in Chesapeake Bay carrying a total of 144 male colonists. They had experienced 'great storms' on the way but arrived safely to found the settlement of Jamestown. They would suffer many deaths and hardships over the next few years, but under the leadership of John Smith they founded the Commonwealth of Virginia, the first successful permanent English speaking colony in what later became the USA. It took off economically when it began to produce tobacco and import slaves to work the fields.

To the north, another group arrived at Cape Cod in the *Mayflower* in 1620. Unlike the Virginia adventurers they were puritans seeking religious freedom and they founded the first settlement of what later became New England. By 1640 there were similar settlements all along the coast, from New Haven in Long Island Sound to what later became Maine. The division between north and south already reflected what was happening in Britain, with the puritans supporting the parliamentary side in the English Civil War, and the land-owning southerners supporting the King. The Second Anglo-Dutch War saw the capture of New Amsterdam from the Dutch in 1664, and its re-naming as New York, after the King's brother. The southern colonies of Carolina were named after King Charles himself. Maryland, sponsored by the Duke of York, was largely Roman Catholic in outlook. Pennsylvania was founded by William Penn, the son of an English admiral, on behalf of the Quakers, but unlike other religious colonies it was prepared to tolerate those of a different persuasion.

The English colonies in both North America and the West Indies were highly successful. The Scots, who shared the same king but not the same parliament, became envious and in the late 1690s they tried to found their own colony at Darien in modern Panama. It was a disaster and in 1707 the Scots were induced to merge their parliament with England's, mainly to get a share in the colonial Empire. From this point in history the Scots traded enthusiastically and successfully, and produced a large number of colonial entrepreneurs and administrators. This fulfilled one of the most important roles of the Empire, to provide employment for the younger sons of aristocratic families. Henry Dundas was a member of the Board of Control of the East India Company in the late eighteenth century and it was said of him: 'As long as he is in office the Scotch may beget younger sons with the most perfect impunity. He sends them by loads to the East Indies, and all over the world'.

The North-West Passage and Hudson's Bay
For centuries explorers dreamed of a new route to the east, north of either Europe or America, which would bring them more quickly to the profitable trade with India, China and the Spice Islands. The English were drawn to the western route, the legendary North-West Passage around Canada. Henry Hudson had already discovered the Hudson River on behalf of the Dutch, when in 1610 he set sail in the *Discovery* from Gravesend in the Thames. He found his way into a huge bay, which was named after him, but was frozen in during a harsh winter. His crew mutinied and put him in a boat, never to be seen again.

Although they had not found the passage they wanted, English explorers opened up the bay, which proved a rich source of furs provided by the native Indians. The Hudson's Bay Company was given a charter by Charles II in 1670, and was supported by his uncle, Prince Rupert. The bay also provided a summer sea route into the interior of Canada. The search for the passage continued into the next century, but any route was commercially unviable.

The American Revolution and Canada
British North America continued to expand in the eighteenth century through free emigration and the importation of black slaves and white indentured servants. The growing cities were

Cook's *Endeavour*

IN 1768 Captain James Cook took command of the *Endeavour*, converted from a collier. She had been built as the *Earl of Pembroke* in Whitby and was similar to the ships in which Cook had served his apprenticeship in the 1750s. She had a flat-bottomed, almost square hull with a shallow draft and good cargo-carrying capacity, which was necessary for exploration. She was simple, with no figurehead and only minimal stern decoration and cabin windows. During her conversion she was given space for a crew of 84, with cabins for officers and scientists in the stern. She had a conventional three-masted ship rig and was 97 feet 6 inches long in the hull with a tonnage of 369.

Carrying a party of scientists led by Joseph Banks, Cook set out to observe the transit of Venus from the newly discovered island of Tahiti, but he took the opportunity to explore the unknown areas of the Pacific. He produced accurate charts of the whole of New Zealand, and discovered a route round the Great Barrier Reef to find the fertile east coast of Australia. He returned home in 1771 after a circumnavigation of nearly three years.

Although he continued to use the North Sea collier type on his voyages, Cook did not sail in the *Endeavour* again. Instead she made three voyages to the Falkland Islands and was sold to continue in the coal trade for another 15 years before being purchased by the French. She ran aground and was broken up off Rhode Island in 1793.

A replica using the original plans and the best historical evidence was completed at Fremantle, Western Australia in 1993 and spends much time sailing in British waters, including visits to her original's home port of Whitby.

BELOW
The 1993 replica of Cook's *Endeavour* in her original's home port of Whitby.

James Cook was the son of a farm labourer who had risen through the ranks of the Royal Navy, to set out on his first voyage of exploration in 1768. In his second voyage (1772–5) he was charged with finding out whether a great southern continent existed in the ocean. He sailed further south than anyone before him and found the edge of Antarctica, but no useable continent. In his third voyage he sailed north to look for the North-West Passage from the Pacific end, but was killed in a scuffle with the natives at Hawaii.

Others followed him. The First Fleet was sent to Australia in 1788 to found the first British colony there. William Bligh had served under Cook and took the *Bounty* to Tahiti to bring home breadfruit. He lacked Cook's leadership skills and his crew cast him adrift in the Pacific in 1789, to make a 4000-mile voyage in an open boat to reach Timor. George Vancouver was more successful in exploring the north-west Pacific coast of America. The sea exploration of Australia was boosted by the colonisation. In 1798–9 George Bass and Matthew Flinders sailed around Van Diemen's Land (Tasmania) and proved it to be an island. Two years later Flinders began a circumnavigation and accurate survey of the Australian coastline but was detained for six years by the French in Mauritius.

The Wars with France

The great wars with France, from 1793 to 1815, were not about empire in the way that the Seven Years War and the War of American Independence had been. Nevertheless, sea power allowed the capture of colonies from the French and Spanish, sometimes more than once as some were given back at the Treaty of Amiens in 1801, to be re-taken in the next war. Ceylon (Sri Lanka) was taken from the Dutch in 1795. The Cape of Good Hope, a crucial stage on the route to India, became a permanent part of the British Empire from 1806. But conquest had its limits. After taking the Cape, Sir Home Popham led an expedition against Spanish Buenos Aires in 1807. As soon as the Spanish realised how insubstantial his force was they overthrew him, and Britain remained weak on the South American continent.

The Victorian Empire

Imperialism had its ups and downs in the course of the nineteenth century. In the early stages it was taken for granted as colonies were acquired almost casually by conquest from a European enemy. It went through one of its least glorious phases in 1839–42, when the East India Company and the Royal Navy fought to open China up to the opium trade, and

HMS *Gannet*

HMS *Gannet* was built at Sheerness Dockyard in 1878 as a sloop to patrol the more remote areas of the British Empire. She had a three-masted barque rig as well as a two-cylinder 100-horse-power engine, as she would not always be close to coal-ing stations. She was of composite construction, with wooden planks on an iron hull, because that was easier to repair using the ship's own resources. She was 170 feet long with a tonnage of 1230 and carried six main guns including two 90-cwt muzzle-loaders.

In 1888, with her sister-ship *Starling*, she bombarded the Dervishes near the Sudanese town of Suakin to relieve a siege. In 1903 she became HMS *President*, a training ship for the Royal Naval Reserve and eight years later she became the *Mercury*, a training ship for boys in the River Hamble near Portsmouth, run by the England cricketer C B Fry. The school closed in the 1960s and the ship was acquired by the Maritime Trust. In 1987 she went to the Historic Dockyard Chatham where her restoration is well advanced.

acquired Hong Kong. In the middle years imperialism became rather unfashionable and the island of Corfu, for example, was given to Greece. The Navigation Acts were repealed and colonies were often considered irrelevant in the new age of free trade. The high profits of India and the West Indies were no longer possible. Patterns of emigration and commerce showed that the USA and Latin America were at least as important as any of the British-held territories, so formal colonial rule seemed unnecessary.

Imperialism came back stronger than ever in the 1870s. One impetus, as in the 'Scramble for Africa' in the 1880s, was to get hold of colonies before others did, for the new rising power of Germany wanted its 'place in the sun' and was envious of British success. Another motive was to facilitate the setting up of stations where warships and merchant ships could take on coal, for the steamship ruled the oceans after 1870. Much of the Royal Navy was stationed in the Empire in these years,

until the 1900s when Admiral Fisher recalled the ships and reallocated the crews to the new battleships which would fight the war with Germany. Imperialism attracted far more intellectual attention than ever before. Conservative politicians such as Benjamin Disraeli and Joseph Chamberlain emphasised the trade possibilities and the civilising mission of the Empire. Socialists such as J A Hobson and Vladimir Lenin saw it as pure exploitation, the last gasp of a dying capitalism.

The great nineteenth-century inventions changed the nature of empire. The steamship meant that it was no longer necessary to follow the trade winds in the Atlantic, or the monsoon in the Indian Ocean. It allowed the building of a fleet of gunboats as an imperial police force. The Suez Canal created new strategic priorities and made Egypt more important than ever. The electric telegraph allowed instant imperial communication. The railway also changed priorities, sometimes away from the sea for the first time. The dream of colonial financier and sometime prime minister of Cape Colony, Cecil Rhodes, of a Cape to Cairo Railway, all in British territory, was a motivation for a new style of inland colonisation.

The Polar Explorers

The polar regions of the globe are either made up of land, as in Antarctica, or covered in ice, which makes them more like land than sea, as with the Arctic. Nevertheless, the Royal Navy has always taken on most of the work of exploring them, since the days when the young Horatio Nelson took part in an Arctic expedition in 1773. In 1847 Captain Sir John Franklin died in the far north in pursuit of the North-West Passage, but it was the Norwegians and Americans who first explored the North Polar region successfully. This left the Antarctic as the last great challenge. James Clark Ross had discovered the Ross Sea and its ice shelf in 1839–43. In 1900 the Royal Geographical Society sponsored an expedition led by Robert Falcon Scott and Ernest Shackleton which got as far as 82° South. In 1912 Scott reached the South Pole only to find that the Norwegian Roald Amundsen had got there first. He and his party perished in the ice on their return journey. Shackleton continued to explore the region and Britain claimed a substantial sector of the land, although it is of little economic value.

The Empire in 1914

By 1914 the British Empire was proud to be the largest the world had ever seen. It had gained nearly 5 million square miles of territory and 90 million more people in the last quarter of the nineteenth century. It had suffered a setback in the South African War of 1899–1902 during the second Boer War and European public opinion was against the British. Nevertheless the 'white dominions' – Canada, Australia, New Zealand and South Africa – had internal self-government with Britain still in control of their foreign policy. India continued to be seen as the 'jewel in the crown' and the independence movement was still weak. The West Indies had declined in importance since the early years

of the nineteenth century and had no great economic value to Britain. The Empire was not yet at its zenith in terms of territory, for after the First World War it would take on new lands as League of Nations mandates. But it was far-flung and difficult to defend and it is doubtful if it was profitable in any real sense. It contributed to the causes of the First World War in that it inspired German envy and emulation, and it would become increasingly hard to maintain in the 40 years that followed.

BELOW

Sir John Franklin's last message, written on a standard printed form and left in a cairn in the Arctic in 1847. It was recovered in 1859.

RRS *Discovery*

ABOVE
The wardroom of the *Discovery* with the table set for dinner.

THE *Discovery* was built in Dundee in 1901, modelled on a whale ship which had been used in the Arctic expedition of 1875–6. Intended to aid the exploration of the interior of Antarctica, she was specially strengthened to take the pressure of the ice and was equipped with laboratories and an observatory. She was powered by a 450-horsepower triple-expansion engine with a lifting propeller but also carried the rig of a three-masted barque.

Her first voyage began in 1901 under Captain Robert Falcon Scott, who discovered King Edward VII Land early in 1902. She remained icebound during the winter of 1902–3 and returned home in 1904. After that she made many voyages on behalf of the Hudson's Bay Company in northern Canada, and resumed polar exploration as a Royal Research Ship from 1923. She was laid up from 1931–6 and then used by the Sea Scouts and the Royal Naval Reserve in London. Transferred to the Maritime Trust, she was taken to Dundee in 1986 where she is open to the public.

RIGHT
The *Discovery* in dock at Dundee.

the merchant navy, and to train them from boy-hood for the Royal Navy. They were given a regular uniform for the first time, and signed on for 12 years, which only started when they reached the age of 18. From this time onwards the Royal Navy seaman was a different animal from the merchant navy man, with his own cul-ture and traditions, and a very rich vocabulary of slang. Ratings with particular surnames, for example, had standard nicknames, as described by Robert Burgess and Roland Blackburn (Petty Officer) in *We Joined the Navy* (1943).

> For instance we have 'Shiner' Wright, 'Dusty' Miller, 'Pincher' Martin, 'Nellie' Wallace, 'Topsy' Turner, 'Pusser' Combe, 'Hookey' Walker… All Thomases are 'Tommo', and all members of the Day clan are 'Happy'. Tall men are alluded to as 'Lofty', short men as 'Stumps', 'Sawn-Off' or 'Shorty'.

The English language has constantly been enriched by the use of sea terms. Some are obvi-ous in origin, such as 'taking the wind out of his sails', or liking 'the cut of his jib'. Others are less clear, such as 'nip and tuck', which originally referred to the extreme ends of a ship, and 'line manager', who was the person who fed out the rope after a whale was harpooned. Even today new terms can be introduced. 'Turning the supertanker round' refers to the difficulty of get-ting things done in a large organisation.

The merchant service exchanged one form of regulation for another. The Navigation Acts had demanded British crews in all merchant-men. These were repealed and owners were free to recruit foreigners, and particularly Indians known as Lascars. But the Victorians were also social reformers and increasingly conscious of safety. Merchant ship officers were now expected to pass examinations in seamanship and navigation. A potential officer would probably start as an apprentice, perhaps in a nautical school in an old hulk. He would work hard to get his 'master's ticket', which allowed him to command a ship, but even that did not guarantee him a command. Some of the more exclusive passenger lines insisted on the ticket even for the junior officers.

This had started to change by 1910, when the navy began to adopt oil fuel, which eliminated much heavy labour. The change was slower in the merchant navy, and many ships were still coal-fired in the Second World War.

The New Seaman

Meanwhile, the Royal Navy seaman's life was changing. Theoretically the press gang was still possible in the 1850s when the Crimean War broke out, but politically it would have been impossible to implement. Instead, it was decided to stop taking the bulk of naval seamen from

RIGHT
A captain's clerk and a seaman in
the 1840s, showing the evolution
of the seamen's dress before it
was adopted as formal uniform in
the 1850s.

There were some who resisted the new order, and they found work on the clipper ships which sailed the oceans until the First World War. One of Joseph Conrad's characters talks about 'chucking in the sea and going into steam'. Crews were smaller than ever in clipper ships; the *Cutty Sark*, for example, never had more than 28 men, so the work was tough.

The British Seaman in the World Wars

When the First World War broke out in 1914 the Royal Navy saw little need to recruit outside its traditional fields. The amateur seamen of the Royal Naval Volunteer Reserve (RNVR) were sent off to fight as soldiers on the Western Front, while the Grand Fleet, manned by highly trained officers and ratings, went to Scapa Flow, where it spent most of the war and saw little action. The officers had been trained at Dartmouth in a system that had too much focus on technical detail and did little to foster initiative; they paid for it at the Battle of Jutland in May 1916.

At the same time another campaign developed, against the U boat. This time merchant shipping was the main target, and more than

ABOVE
Seamen haul on a rope in the
four-masted barque *Parma*, as
photographed by Alan Villiers in
1932. Work like this was common
for sailing-ship men through
the ages.

5500 ships were sunk. The Royal Navy had to look again at its reserves and amateur seamen to set up patrols around the coast. As a reward for its services, the British merchant service was awarded the formal title 'Merchant Navy' and its officers were given a regular uniform, modelled on the naval pattern but with a diamond rather than a curl as the main motif.

Since he signed up for only one voyage at a time, the merchant seaman was particularly vulnerable to unemployment between the wars. Even officers of the Royal Navy found that their career was far less secure than they had hoped, and lost much prestige when the Washington Treaty gave the US Navy parity with the Royal Navy. The sailors of the Atlantic Fleet mutinied against pay cuts at Invergordon in 1931, marking a good deal of underlying discontent about conditions on the lower deck.

In the Second World War the navy expanded more than ever before. Over a million men and women served in it, and by the end regular Royal Navy men were far outnumbered by 'Hostilities Only'. As one cruiser captain put it:

> The Jolly Jack of peacetime was a rare bird indeed.... The wartime sailor, faithfully modelling himself upon his glamorous predecessor, was conscious of the ready-made aura which attached to his own interpretation of the part. ... The model set for them to follow was good and by his exacting standards we were able to run our complicated machines on a very weak mixture of RN spirit!

The navy used its past to good effect. It taught its men to believe, 'I am a British sailor. The British sailor has always been the best seaman, the finest fighter, the hero of the people. Therefore, I am a hero'.

The Merchant Navy had the hardest time of all during the war, suffering casualties of about 25 per cent compared with about 5 per cent for the Royal Navy. Some, especially in the engine room, were lost immediately a torpedo

Greenwich Hospital

ABOVE
The river front of Greenwich
Hospital in 1835, painted by
George Chambers senior.

GREENWICH has long been an important site by land and sea. It is where the Roman road from London to Dover comes closest to the River Thames. The great loop in the river often caused ships to anchor there to await a wind, and it was close to the Royal Dockyards at Deptford and Woolwich. The Palace of Placentia was sited there from late medieval times and was improved by Henry VII and Henry VIII. In the early seventeenth century Inigo Jones built a far more modern building, the Queen's House, on behalf of Anne of Denmark, the wife of James I. It was the first Palladian building in Britain and 'one of the most important buildings in the history of English architecture', according to the architectural historian, Sir Nikolaus Pevsner.

The old palace fell into disrepair and in the 1660s Charles II built a massive block on its site. In the 1690s Queen Mary was distressed to see the condition of some of the sailors released from the navy and she founded the Royal Naval Hospital as a refuge for them, on the model of Les Invalides in Paris and the Royal Hospital at Chelsea as used by the army. Sir Christopher Wren was appointed architect and he designed the hospital in four blocks, incorporating the King Charles building. It became 'the most stately procession of buildings we possess', according to Sir Charles Reilly. Wren's twin domes, with a clock and a wind indicator, can be seen for miles and the buildings provide one of the most prominent landmarks on the River Thames. Internally its highlights include the Painted Hall with murals by Sir James Thornhill, and the Chapel.

The first pensioners took up residence in 1705 and there were 2710 by the end of the Napoleonic Wars in 1815. Governors were distinguished naval figures such as Admiral Hardy, Nelson's captain at Trafalgar. But the building was far too grand for its main use and the pensioners were not allowed to use the Painted Hall. After the Napoleonic Wars the numbers began to decline and it was found more economical to pay them pensions to live outside. It closed in 1869 and became the Royal Naval College for the advanced training of naval officers. The site around the Queen's House was extended by colonnades leading to new wings and it became a school for the sons of seamen. Later the school was transferred to a new site and the buildings were taken over by the National Maritime Museum, which opened in 1937. The Royal Naval College continued with the post-graduate training of naval officers until it, too, moved in 1998. The site was taken over by the University of Greenwich and the Painted Hall and Chapel are open to the public.

Chapter 8
The Age of Steam

Early Vessels

The principles of steam power had been around for a long time before they were translated into reality, and many inventors had the idea of applying it to ships. In 1663 an engine designed by the Marquis of Worcester was demonstrated to Samuel Pepys, and in 1736 Jonathan Hulls produced plans for a paddle tug. But real progress had to await the work of James Watt,

whose inventions, especially the separate condenser, doubled the efficiency of the engine. The paddleboat *Charlotte Dundas* was tested on the Forth and Clyde Canal in 1802, but was rejected on the grounds that her wash might damage the banks. The first successful steamboat in Europe was the *Comet*, which Henry Bell designed in 1812 to ferry passengers from Glasgow to his hotel in Helensburgh on the

Firth of Clyde. After that steam power began to take off. The *Thames* of 1814 made the first steam voyage by sea between Glasgow and the River Thames and the *Margery*, built in the same year, made the first voyage across the English Channel. More than 50 paddle steamers were operating in the sheltered waters of the Firth of Clyde by 1825.

In the first instance steam was useful in rivers, estuaries and short passages across the sea from England to France or Ireland, for example. Steam tugs could be used to tow sailing ships in and out of harbour: the name came from the *Tug* built in 1817 for use in the Firth of Forth.

Iron construction had been tried on the *Vulcan* on the Forth and Clyde Canal in 1819. The *Aaron Manby* was built on the Thames in 1821 and fitted with a 50-horsepower engine. She crossed the Channel to operate on the River Seine. The great leap came in 1838 when Isambard Kingdom Brunel built his *Great Britain* in iron and she subsequently survived a grounding off Ireland which would have wrecked a wooden ship.

Steam Warships

The British Admiralty was not nearly as reluctant to take up steam power as is generally believed. Lord Melville, the First Lord of the Admiralty, did not actually say, 'their Lordships feel it is their bounden duty to discourage to the utmost of their ability the employment of steam vessels, as they consider the introduction of Steam is calculated to strike a fatal blow at the supremacy of the Empire'. In fact he did much to encourage the new method of propulsion. The first naval steamship was built for exploration of the River Congo in 1816 but was apparently not a success. Two ships, the *Lightning* and *Meteor*, were built for the packet service to Ireland in 1821, and the *Lightning* carried the King on a visit to Ireland. Another *Lightning*, built in 1823, served in an expedition to Algiers and later appeared on the Navy List as a warship. There were several intermediate ships until the *Gorgon* appeared in 1835. She was bigger than any of her predecessors at 1111 tons and 800 indicated horsepower, and many more ships were based on her design.

The paddle steamer had several serious disadvantages as a warship. On the open sea, one wheel might be out of the water while the other was deeply immersed, making it very difficult to steer. Furthermore, the wheels took up about a third of the available area for the broadside. This was more important on a ship of the line which relied on several decks of guns, so paddle warships were limited to frigates and sloops, carrying a small number of guns, up to 68-pounders.

The Screw Propeller

The idea of the screw propeller had existed since the time of Leonardo da Vinci but it was of little practical use without an engine. In 1837 the Swede John Ericsson built a vessel called the *Francis B Ogden* with a propeller. Meanwhile the Englishman Francis Pettit Smith patented his own versions in 1836 and 1839, based on the ancient principle of the Archimedes screw. Brunel adopted the screw propeller for his second ship, the *Great Britain* of 1843.

In April 1845, in order to demonstrate the value of the screw propeller, the Admiralty arranged a tug-of-war between the screw-driven *Rattler* and the paddle steamer *Alecto*, of similar size and engine power. Scientifically the experiment was rather dubious but the *Rattler*

duly towed the *Alecto* backwards at a speed of 2.8 knots. The point was made and the Admiralty converted several ships of the line to screws. Paddle ships continued to be used in shallow waters, and where their manoeuvrability could be useful.

Brunel's Ships

Isambard Kingdom Brunel, the son of a French émigré who had built mass-production block mills in Portsmouth Dockyard, was already established as an engineer with the Great Western Railway when he had the idea of extending the line across the Atlantic with a ship, which he called the *Great Western*. In 1838 she had an epic race with the much smaller *Sirius* to be the first to cross the ocean entirely under steam.

In 1843 he launched a much more innovative ship, the *Great Britain*, which was also a success, but he overreached himself with his next ship. It was planned to make a non-stop passage to India, hence its name, the *Great Eastern*. Brunel calculated that only a very large ship would be able to take enough fuel and he designed one of nearly 19,000 tons, five times the size of the largest built so far. She had sails, steam and paddles and was built on the River

ABOVE
The tug-of-war between the *Rattler* and the *Alecto* in 1845.

ABOVE RIGHT
Isambard Kingdom Brunel stands in front of the chains used to launch the *Great Eastern*.

RIGHT
The *Great Eastern* under construction on the Thames opposite Greenwich, with Greenwich Hospital in the background. The ship had to be launched sideways.

Thames opposite Greenwich. It was intended to launch her sideways into the water but it took several weeks in 1857–8 to achieve this. The strain ruined Brunel's health and he died in 1859. The ship was never a success as a passenger carrier but proved useful in laying the first successful transatlantic cable.

Technology and War

The Crimean War (1853–6) was Britain's only engagement with a major European power between the Battle of Waterloo and the First World War. It was something of a misnomer, as the Royal Navy fought against the Russians in the Baltic as well as on the Crimean peninsula. Allied with France and Turkey against the large but inefficient Russian Fleet, the British faced no real challenge at sea, but it was the first major war in which steamships took part, and it provided many lessons. Several steamships of the line took part in the bombardment of Sevastopol in October 1854, while the sailing ships were taken into action by tugs, highlighting the necessity for all warships to be steam powered. Shells from the Russian forts during the campaign did much damage to the allied

SS *Great Britain*

Probably no ship in history can claim so many firsts as the *Great Britain*. Designed by Isambard Kingdom Brunel, she was the first iron ocean-going ship, the first to use a screw propeller on the open seas and the largest ship of her day. She was 322 feet long and of 2936 tons and was built in a dry dock in Bristol. She was launched in 1843 by Prince Albert, a great supporter of new technology. She had a four-cylinder engine driving a 15½-foot diameter propeller and could make a speed of 11 knots. She also had six masts, all fore-and-aft rigged, except the second one. She could carry 260 passengers in single and double cabins.

Brunel took her to London to show her off for six months; then she made her first voyage to New York in under 15 days in August 1845. The following year she was stranded at Dundrum in Ireland when outward bound from Liverpool and remained there for eight months until she was hauled off and repaired. Under new management, she began to carry emigrants to Australia and in 1855–6 she took troops to the Crimean War before resuming the Australia service.

In 1876 she was laid up at Birkenhead and in 1882 her engines were taken out, her hull was sheathed in wood and she was used as a sailing cargo vessel between Britain and San Francisco. In 1886 she was partly dismasted and laid up in the Falklands Islands, the graveyard of many casualties of Cape Horn. She served as a storage hulk for many years until an appeal, launched by a group led by the naval architect Ewan Corlett, raised enough money to tow her back to Bristol, where she arrived in July 1970, on the anniversary of her launch. She was gradually restored to her original condition, based on careful research, and is open to the public.

BELOW LEFT AND RIGHT
The bow and stern of the *Great Britain* in dry dock in Bristol, showing the early design of propeller.

fleet, demonstrating the obsolescence of wood-en-hulled warships.

By the end of the decade Britain and France were rivals again and were looking at the use of iron to armour ships. The French took the lead with the *Gloire*, launched in 1860. The British followed with the larger *Warrior*, starting a new age of armoured warships. Across the Atlantic, the American Civil War of 1861–5 had its lessons too, although Europeans did not always pay attention to them. They did notice the effect of armour and the use of Ericsson's turret guns in the famous battle between the *Monitor* and the Confederate *Virginia*. This posed a problem for warship designers, as the turret would greatly affect the stability of a seagoing warship. Captain Cowper Coles of the Royal Navy believed he could fit them in a sailing ship by mounting them on a low deck with a flying deck over it. His *Captain* was lost in the Bay of Biscay with him on board not long after her completion in 1870, and the idea died with him. The next step, taken by Sir Edward Reed in the following year, was to build a ship with turrets but no sails. HMS *Devastation*, was in a sense, the first modern warship.

Compound and Triple Expansion

Early steam engines operated at quite low steam pressure in their boilers, and burned a large amount of coal for a given horsepower. High-pressure steam was possible as boilers improved, but it was largely wasted until the invention of the compound engine. This used the steam first of all in a high pressure cylinder, then again in a low pressure one. The compound engine doubled fuel efficiency and became common in merchant ships from the 1850s.

The next step was to add a third or intermediate cylinder to produce the triple-expansion engine, which was even more efficient. It was developed by John Elder on Clydeside and in 1881 it was fitted to the *Aberdeen* for the route to Australia. There were more than 150 triple-expansion engines in service by 1886. The Royal Navy began to adopt triple-expansion engines in the mid 1880s, and the Atlantic liners *City of Paris* and *City of New York* were built with them in 1888. Fuel efficiency had been vastly increased, making ocean steamship routes a practical possibility.

The Steel Warship

The building of the *Warrior* and then the *Devastation* sparked off a new naval revolution. Rifled, breech-loading guns became standard in the Royal Navy from the mid 1880s. They fired explosive shells rather than solid shot, offering much greater range and destructive power. Ship designers replied by increasing the amount of armour plating and developing new types of steel to make it more efficient.

After the Battle of Lissa between the Austrians and the Italians in 1866, ram bows

HMS *Warrior*

HMS *Warrior* was launched into the River Thames at Blackwall in 1861. The warship was built in response to the French *Gloire*, but she was larger than her rival and, unlike her, had a hull built of iron rather than a wooden one covered in it. She was 418 feet long, 140 feet longer than the largest wooden ship and 163 feet longer than the *Gloire*. She introduced the concept of an armoured citadel in the centre of the ship, with the bows and stern unprotected. She had a very high length-breadth ratio of 6.5:1, which made her difficult to steer. Her 5267-horse-power engines drove a single screw to give a maximum speed of 14.1 knots. She was rated at 40 guns, most of which were 68-pounders. Her range under steam was short and she carried a full complement of sails on her three masts, with a crew of 700 men. She was the first ocean-going iron warship, and rendered all other ships obsolete, famously being described as 'a black snake among the rabbits'.

The *Warrior* was rated as a frigate because of her single gundeck, and indeed she was intended to run from any strong battleship opposition. She joined the Channel Fleet in 1861 and took part in voyages round Britain to show the flag. But technological change was rapid and she was quickly outclassed. She was refitted several times but could not keep up with the latest ships. She remained as a warship, mostly on reserve and training duties, until 1900 when she was reduced to a hulk as part of the torpedo school at Portsmouth. In 1929 she became an oil jetty in Pembroke Dock and in 1979 she was towed to Hartlepool for restoration to her original condition. In 1987 she was taken to Portsmouth where she was opened to the public at the entrance to the Historic Dockyard.

LEFT
The *Warrior* afloat at Portsmouth showing some of her coppering, a traditional figurehead, the funnels for her engines and her rigging.

were fitted to large warships in the belief that this might develop into the main weapon of the future. In reality they did more damage to friend than enemy, as when the *Camperdown* accidentally rammed the *Victoria* in the Mediterranean in 1893, sinking her with the loss of 358 lives.

Ships such as the *Devastation* and her successors were mostly designed for coastal work, with short range and poor sea-keeping in rough weather. This changed with the *Royal Sovereign* class of battleships of 1891, which had high forecastles to meet heavy seas. Their 11,000-horsepower engines drove them at 16.5 knots,

they were armed with 13.5-inch, 6-pounder and 3-pounder guns and had armour up to 14 inches thick. They set the pattern for development over the next 15 years.

The frigate class became obsolete as all ships from the *Warrior* onwards had a single deck. They were replaced by the cruiser for scouting ahead of the fleet, and protecting British commerce on the high seas. Several different types emerged. The armoured cruiser was sometimes as big as a battleship but with higher speed and less armament. The protected cruiser relied on light armour and the arrangement of its coal to keep out enemy shells.

Smaller cruisers were used as scouts, despatch ships and as leaders of destroyer flotillas.

Obviously the best way to strike a lethal blow against a ship was to hit it underwater. Static mines were used against British warships in the Baltic during the Crimean War, but an even greater threat was developed by the Englishman Robert Whitehead. Working for the Italians, he invented the first 'locomotive torpedo', which could be launched through the water against an enemy ship. The British began to build fast, manoeuvrable torpedo boats of their own, beginning with the *Lightning* of 1876. But the threat of hostile torpedoes remained strong and the Royal Navy had most to lose by the new weapon. In 1892 they ordered *Havock* and *Hornet*, the first 'torpedo boat destroyers', twice the size of torpedo boats and intended to protect the fleet against enemy torpedoes. The ships of this type became larger over the years and were known as destroyers. By 1914 they had almost evolved into general-purpose warships in their own right.

Trade under Steam

By the 1870s, a worldwide system of steam trading ships had been built up, mainly dominated by the British. The opening of the Suez Canal in 1869 transformed the route to India because the passage through the windless Red Sea was unsuitable for sail. Compound and triple-expansion engines meant that merchant ships needed to carry only the vestiges of a sailing rig for use in emergency. Steel began to replace iron for hull construction after 1879 when the *Rotmahama* showed the possibilities on the route to New Zealand.

Two types of merchant ship began to emerge after 1870. The 'liner' was not necessarily a passenger ship, but one which operated on a regular route. Great shipping lines such as the Peninsular and Oriental Steamship Navigation Company (P&O) and Union Castle carried both cargo and passengers. The world was encompassed by British lines, because of their mastery of steam power and iron shipbuilding, plus the amount of capital and seafaring experience behind them, and those of other countries found themselves

pushed into second place. The liner companies operating particular routes held regular conferences to fix fares for different types of goods.

The 'tramp' was not necessarily as broken-down as the name suggests. It probably meant a migratory worker rather than a down-and-out when it was first applied to ships that followed no regular route but picked up cargoes where they could around the world. The market depended on the electric telegraph, which allowed agents to direct the movements of ships at a distance. Coal was the classic tramp cargo but others included grain, ore, cotton, wood or fertilisers. A tramp ship might spend a long and unpredictable period away from home. The *Queen Louise* spent several years in foreign waters from 1899 until early 1904.

Ships by this time were mostly owned by companies rather than groups of small shareholders. Each company worked hard to establish an identity in a competitive market, flying its own house flag from the stern of its ships and painting the funnel in easily identifiable colours: Alfred Holt of Liverpool was well known as the Blue Funnel Line. Many lines gave their ships names that reflected the company, such as the Castle Line, which merged with the Union Line in 1900, whose ships' names ended in 'Castle'; and the Clan Line, founded by Charles Cayzer in the 1870s, whose ships' names took the prefix 'Clan'.

Steamships were also used in the coastal trade, although Thames sailing barges and coastal schooners were still used in some trades. Steam colliers kept London supplied with coal from the north-east. The 'flat irons' were designed with low superstructure and collapsible funnels to pass under the Thames bridges to reach the London power stations. In Scotland, the Clyde puffer was no more than 66 feet 6 inches long so that it could fit into the locks of the Crinan Canal. It carried general cargoes round the Clyde, West Highlands and Hebrides.

Several types of specialised ship developed in the late nineteenth century. Oil tankers were needed for the US oilfields and in Baku in Russia. Originally it was carried in barrels but in 1886 a Newcastle yard built the *Gluckhauf*, the

first specialised oil tanker. The first cargo of frozen lamb from New Zealand was carried by the sailing ship *Strathleven* in 1880. Four years later the *Elderslie*, the first purpose-built refrigerated ship, was launched. As well as the mutton trade with the Antipodes, the frozen meat trade with South America became very important.

New Ports

Increased shipping activity and the use of ever-larger ships demanded new ports, or at least the extension of established ones. London and Liverpool became by far the most important. London dealt mainly with the import of consumer goods, Liverpool with the export of manufactures. Links with railways became increasingly important, especially for passenger ports such as Dover and Southampton: many of the ferry ports were owned by the railway companies. Steam and hydraulic power allowed the installation of cranes in docks, but the loading of ships remained a very inefficient business, which might cause the ship to be in port for weeks. Docks employed mainly casual labour, which caused bad labour relations. In 1889 the London dockers went on strike for a rate of 6d (2½p) an hour, the 'dockers' tanner'. It was the first time that British unskilled workers had organised themselves successfully.

The Royal Dockyards also began to change. The River Thames at Woolwich and Deptford was too narrow to handle the new steamships, and the yards were closed in 1869. Iron warships needed more sophisticated maintenance facilities and the three remaining yards, Chatham, Portsmouth and Plymouth, were expanded about fourfold round great wet docks. With the threat of war with Germany the Admiralty bought land at Rosyth in the Firth of Forth in 1903, but the new yard was not ready for use until 1916.

The dockyards also had the problem of defence against the new steam warships. A Royal Commission of 1859 recommended setting up a ring of forts by land and sea round the three dockyards, known as Palmerston forts after the Prime Minister of the day. They were built at considerable expense and remain as land and sea marks, especially at Portsmouth and Plymouth where they are most visible.

Shipbuilding

The new iron shipbuilding demanded different techniques. In the private shipyards, the boilermakers already knew how to rivet iron plates together and they took on the main work of assembling the hull, leaving the old-fashioned shipwright with the tasks of laying off the lines and supervising the erection. In the Royal Dockyards, the shipwrights made the effort to learn the new skills and remained the dominant part of the workforce.

As iron, steel and engines became more important in shipbuilding, the old yards in areas such as the south of England began to decline, although the last major yard near London, the Thames Iron Works, did not close until 1912. Meanwhile new yards sprang up closer to the iron-working areas, where engineering skills were readily available, and wage and land costs were lower. The Clyde built very few ships before the nineteenth century, although Scott's of Greenock, founded in 1711, was one of the oldest companies in the country. The cousins David and Robert Napier designed steam engines and Robert set up an innovative shipyard in Camlachie, Glasgow in the 1820s. Many of his employees went on to set up their own yards

Newcastle Port

Coal has been exported from Newcastle and the River Tyne since very early times, but the great boom began in the eighteenth century. New techniques such as steam pumps could be used to dig deeper mines, while the growing cities and the use of steam power created demand. From 1702 to 1788, Newcastle-owned shipping increased almost tenfold from 11,000 tons to 106,100 tons. Most of these were colliers. Steam colliers were adopted after the pioneering *Bedlington* of 1841. By 1879 more than 15,000 ships were using the Tyne ports per year, and nearly 10,000 in the port of Sunderland.

Coal 'stalthes' were used to load coal on Tyneside. Each consisted of a railway running downhill from the pit-head to a jetty, which carried a truck out high over the river and the ship. Various ingenious mechanisms were used to tip the truck and its coal into the hold. Often a horse travelled downhill on the back of the truck and then hauled the empty one up the hill. Steam power was applied early on the Tyne, where the pioneering locomotive 'Puffing Billy' was built in 1815 and George Stephenson, the railway engineer, began his career. Docks were built along the Tyne in the nineteenth century, alternating with shipyards. The river was shallow in many places until the 1860s, when a programme of dredging began.

The Clyde was close to the ironworks of Lanarkshire, the Scottish educational tradition produced good craftsmen and draughtsmen, and the newly built up banks of the Clyde provided plenty of suitable sites for yards. Firms such as Fairfield of Govan, Denny of Dumbarton, Barclay Curle of Glasgow and later John Brown of Clydebank became world famous, while Yarrow, builders of destroyers for the navy, moved to Glasgow from the south coast in 1906.

In north-east England, shipbuilders supplied their local market for colliers and tramp steamers. There were also larger yards, which were important on a national and international scale. On the River Tyne, the great pioneer engineer and armaments maker, Sir William Armstrong, set up his yard at Elswick in 1847, moving down river to High Walker by 1913, after the Tyne Bridge made access to Elswick more difficult. Swan Hunter and Wigham Richardson was formed in 1903 by the merger of smaller yards at Wallsend, and built Atlantic liners including the *Mauretania* of 1906. Palmers of Jarrow was founded in 1851 and in later years concentrated on large warships. Its closure in 1933 sparked off a famous hunger march.

Shipyards on the River Wear included Doxford's, which built 'turret ships' with a unique upper hull form, and Hartlepool built many colliers and tramps including a type known as the 'well-decker' because of the arrangement of its upper decks. Smith's Dock was founded at North Shields in 1899 and moved to Middlesborough in 1910. It built steel trawlers and whalers.

On the Mersey, the main shipyards were at Birkenhead across the river from Liverpool. Cammel Laird was the largest in the area, formed by a merger in 1903 from companies that had existed since 1824. The Barrow Shipbuilding Company was founded at Barrow-in-Furness in 1871 to make use of local iron supplies. It was taken over by the Vickers group in 1897. This represented an increasing trend for steel and armament companies to get involved in shipbuilding, to find an outlet for their products.

On a world scale, British shipbuilding reached a peak in 1892 when it produced 81.7 per cent of world tonnage. Output fluctuated from year to year according to the economic circumstances but the general trend was still upwards until 1913, when nearly 200 million tons were launched. However, the German and American industries were beginning to rise and Britain by this time produced only 59 per cent of the world's merchant tonnage.

The Turbine Engine

In 1897, during Queen Victoria's Diamond Jubilee Review of the fleet, a strange craft appeared among the assembled warships, making the incredible speed of 35 knots among the anchored lines. She was the *Turbinia*, designed by Charles Parsons, an engineer. Instead of the up-and-down motion of the reciprocating engine, the turbine engine used a rotary motion created by high-pressure steam. It had already been used to power electric generators, but Parsons was the first to use it at sea. The turbine would soon become the standard power for warships and fast passenger ships such as Channel ferries and Atlantic liners, but ordinary merchant ships continued to use the cheaper triple-expansion engine.

The Great Naval Arms Race

Over the years since the *Royal Sovereign* class of the 1890s, battleships had acquired a miscellaneous collection of weapons – the *King Edwards* of the early 1900s had five different calibres including heavy 12-inch, intermediate 9.2-inch and 6-inch, and small 6- and 3-pounders for use against torpedo boats. The Battle of Tsushima between Japan and Russia in 1905 showed the possibilities of fighting at longer ranges for which a more uniform heavy calibre was necessary. Admiral 'Jacky' Fisher, the dynamic and controversial First Sea Lord from 1904, conceived the idea of the 'all big gun' ship armed with a large battery of 12-inch guns plus lighter guns to fight off torpedo attack. It was to be powered by the new turbine engine, making it faster than existing battleships. The prototype, HMS *Dreadnought*, was hastened into construction and appeared in 1906, a year after her commencement. She rendered all other battleships obsolete, and Fisher was criticised for wiping out Britain's naval superiority.

It was a crucial moment. Germany, united since 1870, was building up a great fleet and the British believed it could only be aimed at them. Britain began to emerge from 'splendid isolation' and seek understandings, if not formal alliances, with France and Russia – the Triple Entente of 1907. A great arms race began, and more than 40 Dreadnought battleships were built in 10 years, with guns increasing to 13.5-inch and then 15-inch calibre. Despite the success of the Dreadnought type, Fisher actually preferred the battle cruiser. This was a successor to the armoured cruiser, with the armament of a battleship, less armour and a longer, narrower hull to give greater speed. Fisher intended them to defend British trade against raiders in a possible war with France, but in practice they became an elite vanguard of the battle fleet.

Naval gunnery was vastly improved in these years and became a matter of public concern, as cartoons appeared in magazines warning the Kaiser of British prowess. Admiral Sir Percy Scott developed training systems and the firing of broadsides allowed for a spread of shot over great ranges. By 1914 the Royal Navy was beginning to fit director towers high in each capital ship, from where the gunfire could be centrally controlled.

Inventors had long dreamed of boats that could travel underwater, and submersibles had seen action in the War of American Independence and the American Civil War. The first practical ones were built by an Irish-American, John P Holland, as a way of reducing British naval power. The British, along with the other naval powers, adopted his design in 1901 and set up its submarine service. The Royal Navy was well aware that the new weapon was at its most dangerous if used against British sea power

Aircraft were also coming into use at sea, only a few years after the Wright brothers' first flight in 1903. The British were not very successful at airship design, but an aircraft was launched from the deck of HMS *Africa* in 1912, naval officers were trained as pilots and the

Royal Naval Air Service (RNAS) was founded.

The arms race did not prevent war between Britain and Germany; in fact it helped to provoke it. When war broke out with the German invasion of Belgium in August 1914 it was very different from the one fought on such a scale nearly a century earlier. Steam power and iron shipbuilding had changed the world in many ways.

ABOVE
Early British submarines passing HMS *Dreadnought* – the new age in naval warfare, as drawn by W L Wyllie.

Royal Observatory, Greenwich

IN 1675 Charles II founded the Royal Observatory at Greenwich near London, and John Flamsteed was appointed the first Astronomer Royal. His task was to take observations of heavenly bodies in order to improve navigation, and in particular to help discover a means of finding longitude. The most prominent building on the site, Flamsteed House, was designed by Sir Christopher Wren and stands on the edge of an escarpment overlooking Greenwich and London.

The north–south axis of the telescopes set up at the Observatory was used as the 'prime meridian' or longitude of 0° 00' 00" for British astronomers and sailors, from which all measurements on earth and in space are taken. This was recognised internationally as the Prime Meridian for the world at a conference in 1884, as the USA had already adopted it and most of the world's charts were based on it. Many astronomical instruments were set up in the Observatory, such as the 'transit circle' telescope built by the seventh Astronomer Royal, Sir George Biddell Airy, in 1850. Its cross-hairs define the Prime Meridian precisely.

Time was also measured from the Prime Meridian. The growth of railways and telegraphs in the late nineteenth century meant that it was no longer possible for each district to set its own clocks by the sun and a common standard, Greenwich Mean Time, was established.

In 1960 the Royal Observatory moved to Herstmonceaux due to light pollution near London, and the original buildings were transferred to the care of the National Maritime Museum. The Royal Observatory, Greenwich now contains a collection of scientific and navigational instruments including several of John Harrison's famous chronometers.

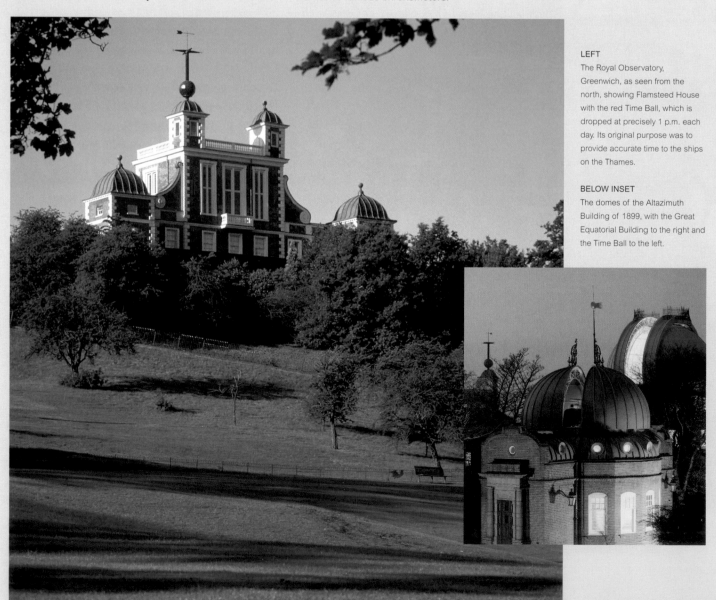

LEFT
The Royal Observatory, Greenwich, as seen from the north, showing Flamsteed House with the red Time Ball, which is dropped at precisely 1 p.m. each day. Its original purpose was to provide accurate time to the ships on the Thames.

BELOW INSET
The domes of the Altazimuth Building of 1899, with the Great Equatorial Building to the right and the Time Ball to the left.

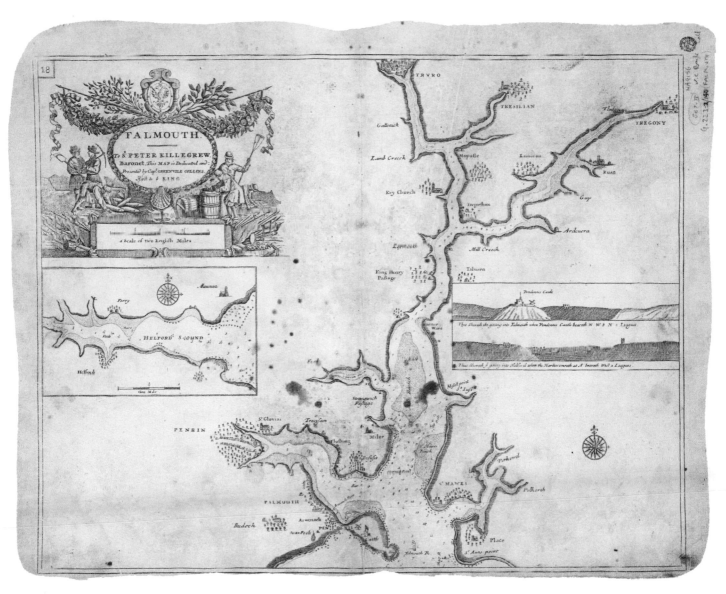

ABOVE
Greenvile Collins' chart of
Falmouth and the River Fal, 1690,
with insets showing views of the
coast, which could be useful
to navigators in establishing
their position.

Hydrographic Department was set up in 1795, initially to collate the work of all chart producers and issue the results to His Majesty's ships. Soon it was producing charts of its own, round the British coasts and much further afield. The most famous of the Hydrographers was Sir Francis Beaufort, the originator of the famous wind scale. Over a period of 20 years from 1835, his department produced more than 1000 new charts covering all the seas of the world. As the British seaborne empire expanded, the Admiralty Chart became established as the standard for world use, by merchant ships as well as warships.

Communication at Sea

Communication between different ships, and between ships and the shore, has always caused specific problems. Flags have long been important, both to establish identity and to pass messages. Prestige ships such as Henry VIII's *Grâce à Dieu* carried a large complement of flags. The *Sovereign of the Seas* of 1637 is depicted with five large flags and at least 28 pennants or streamers, one from each masthead and yardarm. Flags also established the identity of the state. The Union of the Crowns of Scotland and England in 1603 was marked by the first union flag combining the crosses of St Andrew and St George, to be flown from the jackstaff of warships – hence the Union Jack.

Another function of flags was to signal instructions to a fleet. By the Anglo-Dutch Wars of 1652–74, the system was quite sophisticated and used guns as well as flags.

Single and Double Pendants.

Distinguishing Pendants of the Mediterranean Fleet.

										Where hoisted as Single Pendants.	
Neptune	Royal Sovereign	Queen	Victory	Superb	Defiance	Unité	Tonnant	Colossus	Melpomene	Main	Topmast Head.
Lively	Phoebe	Chiffonne	Prince	Renommée	Decade	Kent	Amazon	Aimable	Agamemnon	Fore	
Belleisle	Aurora	Etna	Britannia	Ambuscade	Revenge	Seahorse	Mars	Spencer		Mizen	
Thunderer	Africa		Téméraire	Prince of Wales		Defence	Achille			Starb.	Main the Mizen Topsail Yard Arm.
		Minotaur	Bellerophon	Dreadnought		Polyphemus		Orion		Larb.	
Canopus			Tigre	Donegal	Swiftsure	Sirius		Leviathan		Starb.	
Ajax	Zealous	Hydra	Euryalus	Amphion		Niger	Naiad		Endymion	Larb.	
Conqueror	Juno		Beagle	Weazle	Nautilus	Merlin	Morgiana	Jalouse	Muster	Starb.	
Spartiate		Thunder	Bittern	Termagant	Childers	Eurydice	Pickle	Halcyon		Larb.	
	Nimble			Entreprenante						Cross Jack Yard Arm	

To Sir Thomas Livingston Bart. Captain of His Majesty's Ship Renommée.

Memo. When the double Pendants are used they will be hoisted where best seen.

Nelson & Bronte.

Given on Board the Victory off Cadiz the 29th Sept.r 1805.

London: A.H. Baily & C.o 83. Cornhill.

As soon as the Admiral shall hoist a red flag on the flagstaff at the fore topmast head, and fire a gun, every ship in the fleet is to use their utmost endeavour to engage the enemy in the order the admiral has pre-scribed unto them.

Only pre-arranged messages could be sent and there was no way to reply. New systems using specialised flags were developed in the War of American Independence (1775–83). The great-est breakthrough came with Captain Home Popham's new code of 1799, which provided for a great range of phrases to be sent by two- or three-letter signals, and allowed words to be spelled out for the first time. Nelson used it to send his message, 'England expects that every man will do his duty' at the Battle of Trafalgar. Signal codes were developed for merchant ships to exchange news when meet-ing at sea, and to report their arrival as soon as they sighted port. During the nineteenth century, semaphore and flashing light signals were also adopted. They survived into the radio age, because they could not be detected by an enemy who was out of sight.

Radio was invented by the Italian Guglielmo Marconi, who used it to send a Morse signal from Poldhu in Cornwall across the Atlantic to Newfoundland in 1902. It was soon fitted to the latest passenger liners, for safety and to allow wealthy passengers to keep in touch with business affairs. In 1910 the captain of the liner *Montrose*, bound for Canada, suspected that one of his passengers was the murderer Dr Crippen, and radioed ahead to have the police waiting for him. Two years later radio signals played a complex role during the sinking of the *Titanic* and the rescue of the passengers, although it is claimed that some warnings and distress signals were ignored.

Radio played a part in the First World War, but messages were still mainly transmitted by wireless telegraphy, using Morse code, rather

ABOVE
A page from the signal book used by Nelson at the Battle of Trafalgar, showing the combinations used to identify the individual ships in the fleet. It is signed by Nelson using his Sicilian title of Duke of Bronte.

Denny Test Tank

THE shipbuilding firm of William Denny Brothers was set up in Dumbarton, west Scotland, in 1849. It was always a progressive company, experimenting with new techniques in shipbuilding and design. It built the first practical ocean-going steel ship in 1879, and the first passenger turbine steamer in 1901.

In 1883 it followed William Froude's experiments in Devon by setting up the world's first model test tank in a shipyard. A trolley is used to tow models through the water, and machines create waves and other conditions that ships might encounter. Models are carved in wax on wooden frames, with cutters to reproduce exactly the lines of the ship's plan.

The shipyard closed in 1963 and the test tank, now operated by the Scottish Maritime Museum, is one of the main relics of the great age of Clyde shipbuilding.

than radio telephony using voice. Radio telephony became far more common in the next World War using different wavebands. By the 1970s it could be operated with very little skill and the smallest vessels, down to yachts, were equipped with it. Meanwhile satellite communications allowed the most elaborate messages to be sent to ships anywhere.

Shipbuilding and Naval Architecture

Matthew Baker provided the first known plans of an English ship in 1586, on the eve of the Spanish Armada campaign. Until then shipwrights had worked by 'hand and eye', putting nothing on paper, but the increasing size of ships made this more difficult. In the next century ship design was a matter of solid geometry, as shipwrights used arcs of circles to create the frames of a ship and therefore the shape of its hull. In 1670 Anthony Deane wrote his *Doctrine of Naval Architecture* for Samuel Pepys. The profession of naval architect, however, was slow to separate from the more practical shipwright who actually cut out and assembled the timbers. In theory every apprentice learned both parts of the trade, but in 1664 William Bushnell wrote that master shipwrights taught the skills of design only to a few. The rest learned 'nothing more than to hew, or dub, to fay a piece of timber when it is moulded, to the place assigned'. The French produced many scientific theories of ship design and Sir Isaac Newton took a hand in England, but with little practical effect. By the 1700s ship design was a conservative business, with slow improvements based on previous experience. A School of Naval Architecture was finally set up at Portsmouth in 1811 but closed in the 1830s because naval officers such as Sir William Symonds believed they could design better ships themselves.

Shipbuilders and enthusiastic amateurs had long believed it was possible to predict the performance of a ship by towing a scale model through a test tank, but they lacked the means to translate this into practicality. William Froude, who had worked with Brunel, built a tank at Torquay in 1872, and others followed. Meanwhile naval architecture was becoming established as larger and more advanced ships were built. The first chair was set up at Glasgow University in 1883, funded by Mrs Elder, the widow of a shipyard owner. For the navy, the Royal Corps of Naval Constructors was established in the same year. By 1900 the design of a ship had become a highly scientific business.

The next great revolution came in the aftermath of the Second World War. Prefabrication eventually became standard and the fitting of ships became ever more complex with more electricity and electronics. In the old days it was possible for a foreman on the building slip to alter the run of a pipe, for example, if it got in the way of another. This was impossible with prefabrication where everything had to be planned, so it became increasingly common to design every detail on the computer, leaving no initiative to the workers on the slip.

Nautical Medicine

A ship's medical officer was in a unique position in the days of sail, with virtually no means of calling on help or advice from outside. He had to deal with accidents, battle casualties, the effects of exposure, and epidemics. But not all naval surgeons were well qualified and it was often suspected that they were either young men just qualified, or those who were alcoholics or too incompetent to get a job elsewhere. The situation began to improve late in the nineteenth century, as the great liners began to attract well-qualified doctors.

The surgeon's chest of the *Mary Rose* gives an insight into the horrors of early nautical medicine. It included syringes for urethral injections, bowls for bleeding and tools for cauterising wounds. The middle years of the eighteenth century were perhaps the worst for casualties at sea, as large fleets and squadrons were sent on long voyages before medicine could cope with them. In 1726–7 Admiral Hosier lost more than 4000 men, mostly from yellow fever, in the Caribbean. Fifteen years later three quarters of George Anson's crews were lost during a four-year circumnavigation, mostly from scurvy. This disease, which caused the rotting of gums, the opening of old wounds and a general weakness leading eventually to death, was to become one of the navy's greatest enemies. Eventually James Lind discovered that it was caused by a deficiency of vitamin C, due to a poor diet lacking in fresh fruit and vegetables. During Captain Cook's voyages the men were fed with sauerkraut and 'portable' or condensed soup and the problem largely disappeared. It recurred later in the century until the navy began to issue lime and lemon juice to the men. By 1800 it was almost non-existent.

In battle, the wounded were treated in the cockpit in the bowels of a ship, which could become a scene of horror, as the surgeon of the *Ardent* describes at the Battle of Camperdown in 1797:

Ninety wounded men were brought down from the action. The whole cockpit, deck, cabins, wing berths and part of the cable tier, together with my platform and my preparations for dressings were covered with them. So that for a time they were laid on each other at the foot of the ladder where they were brought down. …

Melancholy cries for assistance were addressed to me from every side by wounded and dying, and piteous moans and bewailing from pain and despair. In the midst of these agonising scenes, I was able to preserve myself firm and collected, and embracing in my mind the whole of the situation, to direct my attention where the greatest and most essential services could be performed.

When Nelson was wounded at Trafalgar he was carried down several decks despite a spinal injury. This horrified a later generation of naval surgeons: 'The man-handling entailed must have greatly exaggerated the shock from his injuries!'

In the Second World War, thousands of doctors were taken from general practice to become naval surgeons, dealing with the effects of stress, exhaustion and overcrowding, as well as battle casualties. In battle the surgeon was advised not to expect to achieve too much, as this extract from an official pamphlet (*The Treatment of Battle Casualties Afloat*) issued to medical officers indicates:

> During action, conditions in the operating theatre are such that no serious surgical work can be attempted; the traditional silence is replaced by a confusing medley of sound – the roar of salvoes and shattering detonations as the ship gives and receives punishment, the din of Fire Parties clearing burning debris and Repair Parties shoring up bulkheads and fixing temporary lighting between decks. There are the added discomfort of fumes, smoke and water, and the ship's evolutions will increase the extent and frequency of her roll and pitch.

In the modern world, nautical medicine is less of a specialised skill. Although doctors are still carried on passenger ships, radio advice is universally available, and serious casualties can be lifted off by helicopter in most parts of the world.

Liverpool Docks

LIVERPOOL was a small town until the eighteenth century, by which time its geographical position gave it great advantages. It was close to the growing industrial area of Lancashire and became its main port as its competitor, Chester, was hampered by the shallow waters of the River Dee. Liverpool had good communication with Ireland and with North America. During the almost constant wars with France and Spain in the eighteenth century, Liverpool ships passed round the north of Ireland and were safer from French privateers than the ships of Bristol, for example.

The tidal flow of the Mersey was strong and docks were necessary if the port was to expand. The first was the Old Dock, which first opened in 1715. Five more docks would be built during the century, and 20 more in the half-century after that.

Gladstone Dock, eventually opened in 1927, was 49 acres in extent compared with 3½ for the Old Dock and 17½ for the next largest, the Canada Dock of 1858. In the centre of Liverpool, the skyline is dominated by the great maritime structures of the Customs House, the Royal Liver Insurance Building and the Cunard Building.

By the twentieth century Liverpool rivalled London as Britain's main port, carrying 27 per cent of national trade in 1913 compared with London's 29 per cent. But Liverpool had only a fifth of the population of London and so was far more dependent on its docks, which began to

decline from the 1920s onwards. Today the Royal Seaforth Dock near the mouth of the Mersey serves as a giant container terminal, which is far more productive than those of the nineteenth century, while others are closed, and the Albert Dock is used for museums, shopping centres and arts complexes.

ABOVE
Liverpool Docks in 1958, close to the end of their heyday. Trafalgar Dock is the nearest one, with Stanley, Collingwood and Nelson docks behind, all dating from the 1830s and 1840s.

Civil Engineering

Early ports were mostly on rivers, improved by building up the banks behind wooden walls. The eighteenth century saw an increased building of enclosed wet docks, where ships could unload behind lock gates away from tide and currents and behind walls to prevent pilferage. The first of these was Greenland Dock on the Thames in 1700, but that was intended for ships under repair or laid up for the winter. The real beginning came with Old Dock at Liverpool in 1715. In London the problem was space rather than strong tides. Ships could often wait for weeks to unload at the limited number of river berths, until the West India Dock was opened in 1802. Others followed rapidly, in London and throughout the country. The major exception

was Clydeside, where open docks, subject to the rise and fall of the tide, were used in the development of Glasgow Harbour. Soon the term 'dock' became synonymous with a commercial harbour throughout Britain, whether enclosed docks were used or not, and the people who worked there were called 'dockers.'

Another approach was to create a new harbour by building breakwaters out into the sea. This was done by John Smeaton at Ramsgate in Kent in the late eighteenth century, as a refuge for ships caught by storms in the Downs anchorage nearby. At Plymouth, a great breakwater was built to protect the Sound for naval ships. It was commenced in 1812 but lost priority with the end of the wars in 1815 and was not completed until 1840.

Canal building raised civil engineering to a new level, with the need to cut through mountains, bridge valleys and build locks. The workers or 'navvies' were later employed on building railways in the second quarter of the nineteenth century.

All the great civil engineers of the eighteenth and early nineteenth century were involved in harbour work. Smeaton worked in the harbour at St Ives in Cornwall and improved the River Lea Navigation near London, as well as building the Eddystone lighthouse and the Forth and Clyde Canal. Thomas Telford worked on more than a hundred harbours, mostly small ones in the north of Scotland. Isambard Kingdom Brunel built a huge dock at Bristol, although the greatest work in that port was the building of the 'floating harbour' by William Jessop. He sealed off part of the River Avon with locks creating a safe harbour, and diverted the main stream around it.

The coming of the age of steam affected harbour development in many ways. Steam and hydraulic cranes could be used both in the construction of docks, and in loading ships within them. Steam-powered diggers excavated the basins and railways and removed the spoil. Steam dredgers were far more powerful than earlier hand- or horse-operated ones, and could clear a channel towards the dock. Ships found it much easier to manoeuvre within the channels. Steamships acted independent of the wind, and even sailing ships could hire a tug to take them in. The Victorian age saw an unprecedented development in the scale and size of harbours; as ships expanded, they demanded ever-larger docks to hold them.

Nineteenth-century humanitarians dreamed of 'harbours of refuge' near the great anchorages, where ships could shelter from storms. They required very long breakwaters, however, and it was only when the navy became interested in the idea of refuges as bases that they were built at Portland and Dover. The one at Peterhead was eventually completed in 1958 by which time the need had long passed. The harbours found good use for other purposes, for the navy, for ferry traffic and for support of the oil industry.

BELOW
A view of Ramsgate harbour from the north showing the breakwaters extending out to sea to create a sheltered space. Behind is the anchorage of the Downs, and some sea bathing can be seen in the foreground.

Chapter 10
Resources from the Sea

Seafood has always formed a major part of the diet of the people of Britain. Shellfish are prolific on some parts of the coast, and easy to collect in shallow water. Ancient rivers were often full of fish, which could be caught by hand, in weirs and traps, or with hook and line. The development of boats encouraged fishing on lakes and in the sea, using hook and line or net. Meat was often expensive and fish gave an alternative source of protein. The medieval Catholic Church forbade meat on Fridays and saints' days and thus increased the demand for fish. The Protestant Queen Elizabeth retained and augmented these laws to create work for fishermen, who could be taken into the navy in time of war.

Local Fisheries

Most fishermen adapted their boats and skills for local conditions, and this remained true well into the twentieth century. Some of the shellfish trades were more like farming than hunting, in that stocks had to be cultivated and conserved. The famous Whitstable oyster fishery was known to the Romans. As late as 1902 it was written: 'the oyster beds at Whitstable are as carefully prepared and maintained though always under water, as if they were flower beds on shore'. The owners of fishing smacks were members of the Whitstable Company of Free Fishers, which had been given a Royal Charter by George III. The crews were mustered daily and allocated six hours' work, often at night, on a section of the beds, hauling dredges over the ground to catch the oysters. In the typical year of 1912, 19 million oysters were landed at Whitstable, more than half the total English production.

Another local fishery was on Loch Fyne, just off the Firth of Clyde. For centuries the fishermen had used drift nets to catch herring for the expanding Glasgow and Clydeside market. In the 1830s the men of Tarbert began to use a new method, misleadingly known as 'trawling', although more correctly called 'ring netting'. They started by surrounding a shoal of herring with a drift net and then hauling it in and within a short space of time began to design nets specifically for the new method. It required a smaller boat and less capital investment than drift netting, but inspired the wrath of other fishermen. In 1851 an act was passed to ban all nets other than drift nets in the herring fishery. The Royal Navy was called in to keep order and there were many confrontations until 1867 when ring netting was made legal.

The Salt and Kelp Industries

It is not only animals that provide foodstuffs from the sea. Salt was a valuable commodity in ancient times, used as a preservative and to give flavour to food. Seasalter near Whitstable in Kent gained its name from the practice, which happened from Roman times until at least 1806. Sea water was collected in four large pans with the rise of the tide, then evaporated to leave the salt. On the coast of Fife, saltpans can still be seen near St Monans, along with the remains of a windmill that generated the power to raise the water into them. The water was then boiled off using local coal. The industry flourished in Scotland after the Union of 1707 imposed high duties on salt.

The kelp industry was almost entirely Scottish, mainly found in the west coast and the Hebrides. Seaweed was collected at low tide and then laid out to dry and burned in a kiln. The result was a kind of salt which was used for bleaching and in the manufacture of soap

LEFT
Robin Hood's Bay, Yorkshire, in the 1940s, with small local fishing boats drawn up on shore among traditional cottages on a rocky coast. Painted by Richard Eurich.

BELOW
Crofters cutting seaweed on the island of Skye in the 1880s. The industry continued on a smaller scale throughout the nineteenth century after its boom up to 1815.

and glass. It was hard and low paid work, which declined after 1815 when new sources were found in other parts of the world.

Cod and Haddock

More than anything else, the cod was the fish that changed the world. It is a large fish, up to 5 feet long. It breeds prolifically and it is relatively easy to preserve by drying and salting. It could be transported round the world to feed the poor, armies on the march or sailors on long voyages.

Cod is a demersal or bottom-feeding fish which breeds in relatively shallow salt water. As early as 1300 English traders were importing fish from Iceland and by 1436 the fishermen of Scarborough were catching cod and ling in northern waters. This was to remain a staple fishery through the centuries. The largest source in the world is the Grand Banks of Newfoundland, and these provided a motive for John Cabot's exploration in the 1490s. For two centuries or so, fishermen from West-Country

ports such as Barnstaple, Bideford and Appledore crossed the Atlantic to catch the fish, cure it on shore and bring it back. Gradually these were supplanted by ships which sailed across to buy the fish from local people. They were small because they had to enter small ports to load a cargo, and they were schooner rigged to allow them to sail close to the wind. They sailed from Bristol and Liverpool and the Welsh harbour of Portmadoc. The trade peaked towards the end of the nineteenth century.

Closer to home, cod and haddock were caught in British waters by line fishing. A long line was up to 300 feet long and had up to 100 shorter lines or snoods attached to it. Each of these had a hook at the end, and baiting them with mussels or lug-worms was a laborious task before the boat set out. On the fishing grounds, a buoy was attached to the loose end of the line, and it was dropped into the water. The boat sailed slowly forward letting the line out and then came back to pick up the buoy and haul in the line, hopefully with many fish on the

BELOW
Wick Harbour during the herring season late in the nineteenth century, with the outer harbour packed full and barrels for salted herring stacked in the foreground.

Excelsior

Excelsior is a sailing trawler built by John Chambers of Lowestoft in 1921 in the tradition of the Brixham smacks of the nineteenth century. She is rigged as a ketch with the aftermast smaller than the foremost one, and with gaff rig. She is of 100 tons and is 77 feet long. She trawled for plaice in the North Sea until 1935 when she was sold to Norwegian owners. She was brought back to England in 1972 and restored by the Excelsior Trust, which refitted her to her original condition as a trawler and makes her available for charter. When not sailing she is based at Lowestoft.

RIGHT
Excelsior sailing on the North Sea. She has been re-fitted exactly as built, and the fish hold has been adapted to accommodate 12 people.

hooks. Shorter lines were used in ports where the catch was sold locally, for example at Sidmouth in Devon. Fishermen there caught mackerel by trailing a single baited line as the boat moved forward slowly.

North Sea Herring

In the seventeenth and eighteenth centuries the Dutch dominated the North Sea herring fishery, much to the chagrin of British patriots who complained: 'Lords of the sea to be we vainly boast, if others boldly fish upon our coasts'. In 1749 Parliament set up a system of bounties to support the fishery, but Adam Smith pointed out that it was 'too common for vessels to fit out for the sole purpose of catching, not the fish, but the Bounty'. A new act of 1786 reduced the bounty to the boat but offered a shilling (5p) per barrel of cured herring. Fishermen continued to use the 'buss', a boat of Dutch origin of up to 80 tons with a crew of 16 or more. They used drift nets as described in 1785.

The drift net floats with the tide and presents a perpendicular wall of netting frequently 1½ miles long and 10 yards deep. The herring meeting this net mesh themselves into it and being caught either by the gill covers or by the body, are hanged and die.

Herring had an almost limitless market from the late eighteenth century onwards. It was first sold to Ireland and the West Indies then to Germany and Russia. The technology remained largely unchanged until the late twentieth century. In 1929 John Grierson discovered the hard life of the men while making his pioneering documentary *Drifters*.

Two miles of nets of every ship, hand over hand agonies of eight hours on end, a dash for harbour in heavy seas, the long labour of unshipping the catch at whatever hour of day or darkness the boat arrives, putting out again, shooting, hauling, seven days out of seven.

Drifting was eventually superseded in the late twentieth century by the use of seine nets or mid-water trawls.

The Rise of Trawling

Fishermen had long been suspicious of the trawl net, which was spread out and dragged along

Reaper

The *Reaper* is a surviving example of a fifie, the straight-stemmed fishing vessel common on the east coast of Scotland in the nineteenth century. She was built by J and G Forbes at Sandhaven on the Moray Firth in 1902 and is 72 feet long. Registered in Fraserburgh as FR958, she operated as a sailing drifter until 1957, interrupted by the Second World War when she was used as a barrage balloon vessel. She is built of wood, and rigged as a two-masted lugger. She was taken over by the Scottish Fisheries Museum at Anstruther and sails round the coast to attend maritime events.

RIGHT
Reaper leaves Anstruther Harbour under sail. The light tower was built in the 1860s to mark the harbour entrance.

the bottom to catch whatever was there. In 1376 they complained of a net called the 'wondychoum', which had a small mesh and would cause 'the destruction of the fisheries in like places'. In the reign of George I an Act of Parliament banned 'any traul-net, drag-net or set-net' of less than 3½-inch mesh.

Early in the nineteenth century, the fishermen of Brixham on the south coast of England developed new methods. Their home in Torbay was a naval base and they designed small boats with a crew of two men and two boys to evade the press gang. By about 1830, some years after the French wars had ended, they began to build much bigger boats using trawl nets for sole. They began to spread along the English Channel and into the North Sea and in the late 1830s they discovered the 'silver pits' about 75 miles off Grimsby, where large numbers of fish could be found in winter. The Brixham trawler design was taken up by other ports such as Lowestoft, Great Yarmouth and Grimsby, and trawling became a standard method in the area. The Sea Fisheries Act of 1868 repealed restrictions on net size.

Trawling under sail required a strong wind just to get the boat and its trawl moving, and life was brutal for the fishermen. Steam power would clearly give a great advantage during trawling, even though early engines were expensive, took up a good deal of space and made it too easy to deplete stocks. The first steam trawler was an old paddle tug, the *Messenger* of 1843, which made a small catch from North Shields in 1877. More began to operate from Scarborough and in 1882 a Grimsby firm built the first two-screw trawlers, which were far more suitable for the open sea. By the end of the decade the sailing trawler was in decline. The steam trawler needed more facilities and the trade tended to concentrate in larger ports, such as Grimsby and Aberdeen.

Fishing Boats

Each fishing port and area had its own style of boat in the days of sail, although they had much in common. Apart from inshore rowing boats, they were propelled by sail. The herring busses of the eighteenth century used the square sail, but after that they were nearly always fore-and-aft rigged, to make the best use of the winds. Smaller ones such as the Essex smack had a single mast; Brixham trawlers and other large boats were ketch rigged with a smaller mast aft. They were invariably built in wood, either carvel with the planks laid edge to edge or clinker with overlapping planks according to size and the traditions of the region. The great majority were open boats until the late nineteenth century when decks were fitted to the larger ones.

In the far north of the British Isles, the Shetland sixern and the Orkney yole are obviously descended from Viking craft, with clinker build and lug rig. In the east coast of Scotland, two main types developed in the mid nineteenth century. The scaffie of the north-east had a steep rake of the bow and stern, whereas these features were almost vertical in the fifie. A Lossiemouth fishermen, 'Dad' Campbell, had the idea of combining the best features of these and produced the zulu in 1879, the year of the Zulu War. The north-east of England used small, square-sterned open boats known as cobles. The Humber estuary produced the blobber, used for eel fishing among other activities. The beaches of Norfolk had light, clinker-built craft, which could be hauled up when not in use. The Essex side of the Thames estuary had

the smack, with a wide stern and a gaff rig. Further up river was the bawley, with a deeper hull. The River Medway had the doble, a double-ended boat with a hold for live fish.

On the south coast, Hastings was another beach port where rather solid lug-rigged boats were hauled up. The coasts of Devon and Cornwall produced many types suited to local conditions, including the Beer lugger from the town of that name, the Brixham trawler which spread into the North Sea, the Mevagissey tosher and the Falmouth oyster dredger. The tradition of the coracle lingered on in parts of Wales, but wooden craft were launched from the beaches of Aberystwyth and Anglesey. The Irish Sea had a very active industry using the Fleetwood smack, the Manx nobby and the Morecambe Bay prawner. The boats of the west of Scotland had to be strong against the winds and tides and they included the sgoth of the Isle of Lewis, with a bowl-shaped hull.

BELOW
The Brixham trawler *Valerian* with all its sails set. From the stern, these are the mizzen sail with the mizzen topsail above; the mainsail and its topsail, the large fore staysail and the flying jib.

Fishing Ports

Fishing ports are even more varied than the boats that sail from them. Some, such as Plymouth, are large cities where fishing is just one industry. Towns such as Grimsby and Fleetwood are centred on long-distance trawling. Others are small villages, which usually develop into tourist centres through time, such as Mevagissey and Mousehole in Cornwall.

A fishing port obviously needs a harbour. Some are simply beaches. Most of the ones we know today were improved in the eighteenth and nineteenth centuries by building breakwaters and extending quays. Brixham has a large breakwater for example, while Peterhead profited from the building of a harbour of refuge intended to protect passing ships from storms. A port needs a fish market close to the harbour, perhaps with ice houses. From the mid nineteenth century fishing ports developed rail links with the great cities, although some of these are

now closed. The first of all was the Canterbury to Whitstable Railway built in 1830, which closed in 1952.

Traditionally a fishing port has a culture of its own, with an important role for women. They mend nets, carry fish on their back to sell it in the streets as the women of Newhaven did in Edinburgh, conduct much of the business and hold a family together in the absence of the men. Fishing ports have a strong sense of independence and resistance to authority and a communal spirit fostered by common grief when a boat is lost.

The Rise and Fall of Whaling

The whale was of great value in the early modern economy, producing oil for lighting and industrial purposes, plus whalebone for corsets and stiffening bags. As with North Sea fishing, the Dutch dominated the Greenland whaling trade until the eighteenth century, when the

British Government recognised the value of both the catch and the men who worked in the trade, and subsidised the industry. The ports of Hull, Grimsby and London became dominant, and by the 1780s whaling had become a very important industry, bringing back 7000 tons each of oil and whalebone per year. The Scottish ports of Bo'ness, Aberdeen and Peterhead entered the trade, and every year there was a gathering of ships at Shetland where they made up their crews from the local population, amid scenes of great drunkenness.

Whaling ships averaged about 80 tons around 1800. The usual technique was to approach the surfaced whale in a small boat and throw a harpoon with a line attached into it. It was then towed to the ship and hoisted across its stern, where it was cut up and its blubber peeled off. The blubber was melted down on shore. Larger British ships participated in the southern whale fishery against the sperm whale, but that was dominated by the Americans.

British whaling declined in the late nineteenth century as the Norwegians began to compete. Harpoon guns, iron ships and steam power were deployed and the Greenland whale was almost hunted to extinction. In the 1860s mineral oil began to replace whale oil. In 1907 the Leith firm of Christian Salvesen set up whaling stations in South Georgia to chase the sperm whale in the Antarctic region and they caught 2350 whales in 1911–12 alone. They gave up whaling in 1963, before it became almost universally unpopular.

Oil and Gas

In 1964, having reached agreement about median lines with neighbouring countries, the British Government began to sell licences to drill for mineral resources in neighbouring waters. The seas were divided into blocks, each one thirtieth of a degree of latitude and longitude in size. British Petroleum (BP) made its first discovery in the West Sole Field off the Yorkshire coast in 1965 and more followed, including the Forties Field, 180 miles east of Aberdeen, in 1970. During the oil crisis of 1973 the Arab governments raised oil prices fourfold, and North Sea

oil became very valuable when it first came ashore in practical quantities in 1977.

The North Sea oil and gas industries deploy very advanced technology, mostly developed by the Americans in the Gulf of Mexico and largely unseen by the people ashore. There are exploration rigs to find the oil. Some are 'jack up' rigs supported by steel girders, which can be lowered to the bottom. They are moved around by giant 'heavy lift' ships. Another type is the semi-submersible rig where most of the flotation is some way underwater, avoiding the effects of the waves. Motions such as pitch and roll can be compensated for but the most disruptive is heave, the up and down movement which can cause drilling to be postponed, despite 'dynamic positioning' which uses power to keep the rig in position. The North Sea is too rough for the other type of rig, the simple drill ship, which floats on the surface in a normal way.

The production rig is much larger and needs a fleet of tugs to haul it into position. One type is made of concrete and uses gravity to let its lower end rest on the sea bottom. Another type is supported by tubes of steel. The platform is held in position by anchors – new types were developed for the purpose, and they are laid

out by tugs. Helicopters take relief crews out to the rigs, and specially designed supply vessels bring equipment. The oil company has to decide whether to lay a pipeline to take the oil ashore or, in view of the distance or the state of the sea bottom, it is easier to put the oil directly into tankers.

The oil is brought ashore in places such as Sullom Voe in Shetland, Flotta in Orkney, Cruden Bay near Aberdeen and Graythorpe on Teeside. Pipelines transport it to the refineries such as Grangemouth on the Forth. Old ports

such as Aberdeen and Peterhead found a new lease of life in supporting the industry, while in the south Great Yarmouth provides support for the gas fields. North Sea oil production peaked in the mid 1980s at around 125 million tons per year, but gas continued to rise into the 1990s. There are hopes that new fields to the west of Shetland might revive the oil industry, but many critics say that Britain failed to benefit from the boom – that the money made by governments was frittered away while Norway raised herself to a new economic plane, that British firms did not produce as much of the goods and equipment as they might have done, and that the British public was indifferent.

Declining Resources

Between 1958 and 1976 Britain had three 'Cod Wars' in which the Icelanders succeeded in raising their fishing limits from 3 to 200 miles. This was the beginning of a movement to redefine the 'ownership' of the high seas round a particular country, and a growing awareness that the seas, though vast, are not infinite. Modern fishing boats, usually trawlers, are too efficient and sweep up vast quantities of fish, so increasing regulation is required, however controversial the methods by which it is executed.

Meanwhile, there are plans to find new uses from the sea, particularly with regard to energy production. So far tidal barrages and wave machines have not materialised in significant numbers. Wind farms are deeply controversial and will never provide more than a tiny proportion of Britain's electricity, but they do not consume any natural resources. In the twenty-first century the sea will continue to be as important as ever as a supplier of food and energy.

BELOW
Oil support vessel *Balblair* sails away from a North Sea rig, by Geoff Hunt RSMA. (Reproduced by kind permission of the artist)

Chapter 11
The Age of Emigration

For nearly 500 years the seas provided the main routes for mass movements of peoples. Between Columbus's discovery of the route to America in 1492, and the development of jet travel in the 1950s, millions of people made long one-way voyages by sea to start new lives. The continents of North and South America and Australia, the islands of the Caribbean and New Zealand and the region of South Africa were re-populated. The native peoples were dispossessed and marginalised, creating an uncomfortable legacy that has yet to be reconciled in many of these areas.

Sea travel over oceans was dangerous and uncomfortable and it was not undertaken lightly. Many emigrants, such as African slaves or British convicts, had no choice in the matter. Others, such as the Pilgrim Fathers, fled from religious repression. Some, such as the Irish famine emigrants, were escaping dire poverty. Of willing emigrants, the early generations were usually adventurers, such as the first colonists

of Virginia or the Gold Rush migrants to Australia. It was only in the late nineteenth century that respectable tradesmen began to emigrate to better themselves.

Voyages to America

The early travellers, such as those who sailed to Virginia in 1607 in the *Susan Constant* and her companions, suffered great hardship even without storm or piracy. These colonists were all men, but many women went to Virginia at a later date. The next great voyage was in 1620, when the group of Puritans, known to history as the Pilgrim Fathers, crossed the Atlantic in the *Mayflower*. Despite the name they included many women, to try to create a balanced society from the outset.

As new colonies became established on the east coast of North America, many more emigrant ships set out. There were no specialised

passenger ships in those days, and even paying passengers travelled in much discomfort. Mrs Janet Schaw sailed from Scotland in the *Jamaica Packet* in 1774.

> Our bed-chamber, which is dignified with the title of State-room, is about five feet wide and six long; on one side is a bed fitted up for Miss Rutherford and on the opposite side one for me. Poor Fanny's is so very narrow that she is forced to be tied in to prevent her falling over.

But other passengers suffered far worse conditions.

> I ought not to complain, when I see the poor Emigrants, to which our living is luxury. ... They have only for a grown person per week, one pound neck beef, or spoilt pork, two pounds oatmeal, with a small quantity of bisket.

Some travelled as convicts, sentenced to a term as an 'indentured servant' as an alternative to the gallows at home. Others were fleeing from dispossession. In the Highlands of Scotland after 1746, clan chiefs were often keen to get rid of excess tenants and sometimes chartered a ship to take a party to America. In 1776, 5,547 left the tiny island of Gigha.

The Colonisation of Australia

In 1787 a fleet of 11 ships sailed from England carrying more than 1000 people including 746 male and female convicts. The British Government's aims were fourfold – to get rid of its 'criminal class', to found a new society, to establish a base for colonising the Pacific and to open up new sources for raw materials. The First Fleet landed at Botany Bay, previously discovered by James Cook and Joseph Banks and recommended as a suitable site by Banks, but rejected it in favour of Sydney Cove a little further up the coast. Many more ships left Britain in the next three decades and often the convicts lived in horrific conditions for several months. Thomas Milburn and his companions were:

...chained two and two together and confined in the hold during the course of our long voyage...we were scarcely allowed a sufficient quantity of victuals to keep us alive, and scarcely any water. ...when any of our comrades that were chained to us died, we kept it a secret as long as we could for the smell of the dead body, in order to get their allowance of provision...

Conditions improved after 1815 and the death rate per voyage fell from 1 in 31 to 1 in 122, but many more people were transported – 78 ships carried more than 13,000 people between 1816 and 1820. Transportation to Tasmania continued until 1853.

The Emigrant Boom

In the second quarter of the nineteenth century, emigration from the British Isles rose dramatically. Less than 300,000 people left between 1835 and 1839, nearly half a million in the succeeding five years and more than a million from 1845 to 1850. One reason for the rise was extreme poverty. In 1845 and 1846 the Irish potato crop failed, leaving most of the population starving. Many thousands emigrated across the Atlantic, mostly via Liverpool. After some time living in squalid cellars, they found passages in grossly overcrowded ships to New York. Most had little idea how wide the Atlantic was and expected to sight America daily on a voyage that might take weeks.

Gold was discovered in New South Wales and Victoria in 1851 and by the end of the year the news had spread around the world. The new clipper ships were immediately chartered, both to export gold from Australia, and by prospectors in Britain and America who wanted to get there as fast as possible, regardless of cost, discomfort or danger. By 1853 a steerage passage from London to Melbourne cost £25 and a first-class passage cost up to £80, but the new ships could get there in less than 100 days.

The idea of emigration picked up a great deal of intellectual support during the nineteenth century. The economist, Thomas Malthus, suggested that a crisis of over-population was approaching. Philanthropists such as Robert Owen attempted to found utopian settlements in America. Edward Gibbon Wakefield tried to reproduce an idealised version of English society in New Zealand, but was overwhelmed by mass migration. The British Government often gave financial assistance to emigrants within the Empire, as did colonial governments such as Queensland. Skilled workers, single women and domestic servants were in great demand and a suitable family could cross the world for a few pounds. More than 21 million people left the British Isles between 1815 and 1912, sometimes at the rate of more than half a million a year.

The Transatlantic Steamships

After the classic race between the *Great Western* and the *Sirius* in 1838, steam voyages across the Atlantic became a practical possibility. The British Government opened the Post Office packet service to private enterprise. A mail contract demanded a regular service. It guaranteed a certain amount of revenue on a route, which could be supplemented by carrying passengers and freight, but penalties were severe. In 1839 Samuel Cunard agreed to pay £500 for every 12

hours his ships were late. This encouraged the development of shipping lines with several vessels to maintain the service, and steamships were necessary to maintain the timetable. Cunard outbid Brunel and his associates to get the Atlantic contract and founded his famous shipping line. His aim was not to provide luxury travel, but cheap services for emigrants.

Charles Dickens did not enjoy his voyage on his first transatlantic trip in Cunard's *Britannia* in 1842.

> ...she stops, and staggers, and shivers, as though stunned, and then, with a violent throbbing at her heart, darts onward like a monster goaded into madness, to be beaten down, and battered, and crushed, and leaped on by the angry sea...in playing whist we are obliged to put the tricks in our pockets, to keep them from disappearing altogether; and that five or six times in the course of every rubber we are flung from our seats, roll out at different doors, and keep on rolling until we are picked up by stewards.

He returned by sailing ship and did not go back to America until conditions were much improved in 1867.

Robert Louis Stevenson travelled to New York in the emigrant steamer *Ethiopia* in 1888. When he first saw the ship anchored in the Firth of Clyde he was impressed by her size, although she was much smaller than the ships that would follow.

There she lay in mid-river, at the Tail of the Bank, her sea-signal flying: a wall of bulwark, a street of white deck-houses, an aspiring forest of spars, larger than a church, and soon to be as populous as many an incorporated town in the land to which she was to bear us.

Stevenson travelled as a second-class passenger in a cabin, but spent his time with the lowest class of passengers, in the steerage. He observed the class distinction that was becoming stronger aboard passenger liners.

Stories and laughter went around. The children climbed about the shrouds. ...down sat a fiddler in our midst, and began to discourse his reels, and jigs, and ballads, with now and then a voice or two to take up the air and throw in the interest of human speech.

Through this merry and good-hearted scene there came three cabin passengers, a gentleman and two young ladies, picking their way through with little gracious titters of indulgence, and a Lady-Bountiful air about nothing, which galled me to the quick.

The Great Liners

In the last decades of the nineteenth century the transatlantic liner became a symbol of technological progress and national prestige. There was a continuous growth in size from 1888, when Inman Line's *City of Paris* and *City of New York* were the first with twin screws, and reduced the voyage time to less than six days. This sparked off an intense international rivalry between the French, Germans and Americans. The Germans had their first successful prestige ship in the *Kaiser Wilhelm der Grosse* of 1897, which quickly won the Blue Riband for the fastest crossing of the Atlantic.

BELOW LEFT
The propellers of the liner *Lusitania*.

BELOW
The Louis XIV restaurant of the *Aquitania* of 1914, photographed by Bedford Lemere. Only first-class passengers were allowed to experience the splendour of the salon.

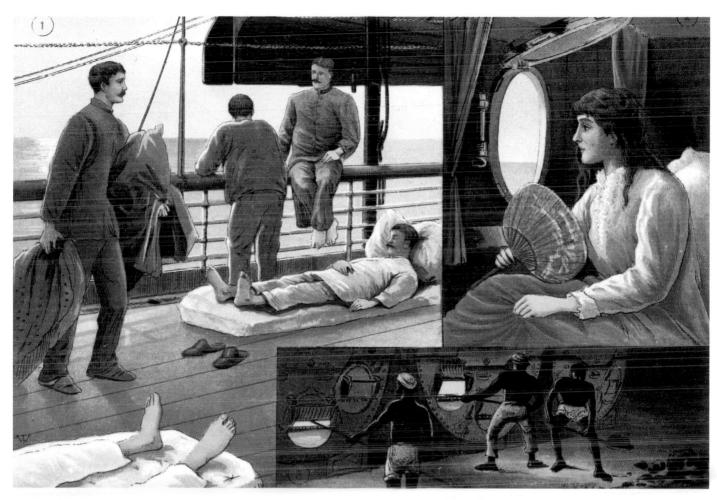

The British were humiliated in Queen Victoria's Jubilee year, but Charles Parson's turbine engine appeared at the same time. Cunard was awarded a British Government subsidy of £2.6 million towards the cost of two new ships, the *Lusitania* and the *Mauretania*, and £75,000 towards the annual running costs. At nearly 38,000 tons, they were more than 25 per cent bigger than their nearest competitor, the German *Kronprincessen Cecilie*. They were the first with turbines, giving a speed of 25 knots compared with 23.5 for the fastest ships with triple- or quadruple-expansion engines. Their first-class accommodation was the last word in seagoing luxury. It was said of the *Mauretania*: 'Never has the interior of a ship had more careful thought bestowed upon it, nor has such an earnest desire after purity of style been manifested'. Cunard's rival, the White Star Line, launched the *Olympic* in 1910 and the ill-fated *Titanic* in 1912, increasing tonnage by 40 per cent, although their ships were slower than Cunard's. The Germans built

the *Imperator* in 1912 and the *Vaterland* in 1914. Cunard's *Aquitania* made her maiden voyage in May 1914. The best of the pre-war liners, she was beautifully fitted, with lounges in the style of the Painted Hall at Greenwich, a French chateau and Robert Adam.

The Routes to the East

P&O started with the mail contracts to Spain and Portugal in 1837. It expanded to take passengers to Egypt, where they travelled overland to join another steamship in the Red Sea to journey on to India. After the Suez Canal opened in 1869 they took passengers all the way to India and Australia, with connections to New Zealand and across the Pacific. P&O offered a very different voyage from Cunard. It took much longer but offered some chance to see the sights of the Mediterranean and Egypt, and P&O tried to make it as distinctive as possible, with a good social life on board. Most passengers were first class, travelling to India as

Queen Mary

IN 1930 work began in John Brown & Co.'s yard in Clydebank on a new Cunard Atlantic liner, the first major one since the First World War. The Great Depression caused many difficulties and the government forced a merger between Cunard and White Star before it gave a loan to complete the great ship, then known by her yard number of 531. Launched by the wife of King George V in 1934 and named *Queen Mary* after her, the ship became a symbol of hope and luxury amidst the despair and hardships of the Great Depression. She also represented national prestige, in competition with the French *Normandie*. It was said at the time: 'The French built a beautiful hotel and put a ship round it. The British built a beautiful ship and put a hotel inside it'. The *Queen Mary* was more than 1000 feet long, with a crew of 1101 and 776 first-class passengers, 784 tourist-class and 579 third-class.

She arrived in New York for the first time on 1 June 1936, and made many round trips to New York before war began in 1939. Her sister, *Queen Elizabeth*, was not completed until 1940 and both ships, minus their luxury fittings, ferried millions of troops about the world during the war and its aftermath. The *Queen Mary* carried a record number of 16,683 passengers and crew in July 1943. She also took Winston Churchill and his staff on several voyages to meet President Roosevelt. In October 1942 she accidentally rammed and sank the British cruiser *Curacoa* off the north of Ireland.

After the war she resumed the Cunard livery and spent more than 20 years as one of the most popular liners on the Atlantic run. By 1967 she was outdated and feeling the effects of competition from the air. She sailed to Long Beach in California where she has been fitted as a floating hotel, museum and conference centre.

ABOVE
The *Queen Mary* in John Brown's yard in Clydebank in March 1936.

army officers, colonial officials or businessmen. Second class was mainly used by servants and missionaries. Compared with the Atlantic route, only a trickle of passengers went to India. The rank and file of the army went by troopship, many of them run by the British India Steam Navigation Company.

Emigrants continued to go to Australia under sail even after the Suez Canal made the steamship voyage practical in 1869. The *Otago*, very similar to the *Cutty Sark* in size and construction, left the River Clyde in 1884 carrying nearly 400 people bound for Queensland. Conditions were very cramped on board. The Hunter family consisted of two adults and three children, which counted as 3½ 'statute adults', with each child as one half. They had 'two beds, the one immediately above the other, 6 feet long by 3 feet 3 inches wide, with a ceiling height in the upper of 3 feet 9 inches and the under 33 inches'. The upper berths were preferable, because they had air and light from 7-inch portholes in the deck. The family also had a sitting space 3 feet 3 inches long and 30 inches wide, with a 9-inch bench, which also served as a locker for mess utensils, and a 10-inch table. 'What a "wee hoose" for our family, and what strange surroundings!' commented Mr Hunter. The voyage took four months, and eight of the passengers died during it.

The Decline of Seaborne Emigration
In 1921 the USA passed the Quota Acts restricting immigration, which removed the need for

the crowded steerage of the transatlantic liners. Cunard, with a reputation for cheap emigrant passages, was forced to reinvent itself as a luxury line and increase the first- and second-class accommodation on its existing liners.

Already there was rivalry from aircraft on some of the passenger routes. The Atlantic was a difficult ocean with no stopping places en route, and early aviators such as John William Alcock and Arthur Whitten Brown, and Charles Lindberg became heroes when they crossed it by air. In 1932 the Germans began an airship service which ended with the tragic and highly publicised loss of the *Hindenburg* in 1937. The Americans launched a flying-boat service in 1939, while the British used flying boats, with numerous stopovers, on the route to India. The Second World War changed the picture completely. Hundreds of runways were built throughout the world to provide the initial infrastructure, while long-range bombers could be converted to airliners. Two more developments – the jet engine and the pressurised cabin – made fast, long-distance travel a practical possibility. In the late 1950s the Boeing 707 and its rivals and successors made economic transatlantic travel possible.

Transatlantic sea passenger services ended in 1973, and air travel was already beginning to dominate other routes, such as Britain to Australia. The great liners, including the *Queen Elizabeth 2*, which had only been launched in 1967, were converted to cruising.

Australia remained open to British emigration long after the United States, and assisted passages were revived to encourage suitable people. At the same time, there was some migration in a different direction, initially by sea. The first party of West Indian immigrants arrived in Britain in 1948 in the *Empire Windrush,* and others came from India and Pakistan in the 1950s, until immigration was restricted in 1961, just as air travel was beginning to take over.

It was not the end of population movement by sea. Western countries increased their barriers to immigration as the economic position of many in the Third World became more desperate. The situation was ripe for illegal immigration, in conditions that were even more squalid than those of the mid nineteenth century. Even today, would-be immigrants are found dead inside containers at ports such as Felixstowe and Dover, and there is no way of knowing how many make the voyage successfully.

Chapter 12
Wreck and Rescue

The British coast has many hazards, with rocks round much of the coast. Those that protrude above the water are less dangerous than those which are just below it, or are covered at high tide. Among the most dangerous are the Eddystone Rocks, on the main route into Plymouth, and the Bell Rock off Arbroath in Scotland, which is covered for half of each tide. Sandbanks are almost as dangerous. They are low-lying, difficult to detect and often shift

with the effects of wind and tide. The most notorious are the Goodwins off the coast of Kent, where hundreds of ships have been lost over the centuries. Sailing ships found it difficult to get off sandbanks once they were aground, and their wooden hulls would be pounded to pieces by the waves. A routine manoeuvre put the 74-gun *Invincible* on the Horse Sand off Portsmouth in 1758. She was almost towed off by her boats, but a change in

RIGHT
A print showing the Great Storm of
November 1703, with ships being
driven from the Downs anchorage
on to the Goodwin Sands.

RIGHT
A print showing the Great Storm of
November 1703, with ships being
driven from the Downs anchorage
on to the Goodwin Sands.

ABOVE
The wreck of a ship on a rocky
coast in the mid-nineteenth
century, by Samuel Walters. The
lee shore was one of the seaman's
greatest dreads.

the wind drove her back again and she broke
up slowly over several days.

Another hazard is the changeable weather.
Summer does not guarantee an absence of
storms, and winter can bring severe ones. Early
navigators became expert at predicting weather
by looking at cloud formations, and used old
rhymes: red sky at night was indeed 'the sailor's
delight' as it often meant that high pressure and
good weather was approaching from the west.
Its opposite, red sky in the morning, meant that
high pressure was moving away and low pressure and stormy weather would probably move
in. On a more scientific level Robert Fitzroy,
who had commanded the *Beagle* during Charles
Darwin's famous voyage, set up the first weather forecasting service in 1861. He used the
barometer and the telegraph to prepare 'synop-
tic charts' and set up storm cones in the ports
to warn fishermen. The introduction of radio
made the whole process much easier. Weather
ships were placed in the Atlantic to report on
patterns approaching Europe, until the use of
satellites made them unnecessary. Even in recent
times, the Fastnet Storm of 1979 caused the loss
of 17 yachtsmen's lives when a depression unex-
pectedly deepened.

According to legend, the work of nature was
sometimes assisted by man. Wreckers, who
deliberately placed false lights to lure ships to
destruction, are commonly believed to have
operated in remote areas of south-west
England. There is no way of knowing how
often this happened, but regulations were cer-
tainly made against it. Local people benefited
by looting cargoes after a ship was wrecked. In
1753 when a foreign ship was wrecked on
Thurlestone Sands in South Devon, it is said
that 10,000 people gathered round and were
dispersed by troops. In 1775 the West Indiaman
Chanteloupe was wrecked in the same area and
local tradition has it that a lady was washed
ashore alive but was murdered for her jewellery.

The shore seems comforting to a landsman,
but to the seaman it also brings a hint of danger. A square-rigged sailing ship could make little progress against the wind, and none at all if
a gale was forcing it sideways, creating 'leeway'.

Every sailor feared a 'lee shore', when a wind might drive him into it without any escape. In December 1811 the 98-gun *St George* and the 74-gun *Defence* were driven on to the Danish coast with the loss of nearly 1400 lives.

Fire was an ever-present danger to a wooden ship. Charles I's great *Sovereign of the Seas* was destroyed by a lighted candle and the carelessness of a shipkeeper in 1696. The 100-gun first rate *Queen Charlotte*, flagship of the mighty Mediterranean Fleet, caught fire and blew up with the loss of about 700 lives. Poor navigation was another hazard, either for ships picking a path through intricate sandbanks, or for those approaching from the Mediterranean or across the Atlantic.

Sea Disasters under Sail and Steam

Many great shipwrecks became etched on the local or national memory. The capsizing of the *Mary Rose* was a national disaster at the time, even though it eventually led to a great boost in nautical archaeology in the twentieth century. The Great Storm of 1703 – a hurricane with winds of up to 80 miles per hour – swept across southern England, destroying Eddystone lighthouse and causing the deaths of about 8000 sailors, including the crews of four ships of the line driven on to the Goodwin Sands. The capsizing of the 100-gun *Royal George* at Spithead in 1782 inspired Cowper's poem *Toll for the Brave*. In August 1848, 900 fishing boats based along the coast from Wick to Peterhead were caught in a storm. The water was too low to let them enter Wick Harbour and 124 boats were lost. In October 1881, 129 fishermen from the small Scottish port of Eyemouth were drowned, along with 62 from other parts of the coast.

In those days only the great disasters hit the headlines, and many passed almost unnoticed. During the years 1793 to 1799, it is recorded that 2385 British merchant ships were lost at sea and 652 more were driven on shore. In 1868 more than 2500 vessels were wrecked or damaged on the British coast. Samuel Plimsoll reported that nearly half were 'unseaworthy, over-laden or ill-founded vessels of the collier class chiefly employed in the coasting trade'. He blamed insurance, which meant that owners had little fear of loss, and even caused

Titanic

THE White Star liner *Titanic* was built in the Belfast shipyard of Harland and Wolff. She was 852 feet long and her 50,000-horsepower engines could drive her at 24 knots. With her sisters *Olympic* and *Britannic*, her first-class accommodation represented the peak of luxury afloat. She had accommodation for 1034 in first class, compared with 510 second and 1026 third. With her 15 watertight bulkheads, the press considered her unsinkable.

She left Southampton on 10 April 1912 on her maiden voyage, carrying Bruce Ismay, managing director of the line, and other wealthy passengers, although she was not filled to capacity. Captain Edward J Smith took the ship well north and radio warnings of icebergs were ignored. Late on 14 April she struck one, breaching six of her bulkheads. She began to sink slowly as passengers and crew took to the lifeboats. But due to outdated regulation, spaces were provided for only a third of the 3500 people she could carry if fully loaded. The officers applied the policy of 'women and children first' and gave priority to first-class passengers, so some lifeboats were not filled. The liner *Californian* did not answer her radio distress calls but many survivors were picked up by Cunard's *Carpathia*. At least 1500 people were lost. The wreck was found by Robert Ballard in 1985.

The *Titanic* is one of the most enduring stories of the twentieth century, with lasting appeal to novelists and film directors. The huge, technologically advanced, class-divided, arrogant society, ignoring warnings and steaming into disaster, seems like a metaphor for the war which engulfed Europe two years later.

ABOVE
The ill-fated *Titanic* proceeds to sea with the help of a tug. Models and artefacts relating to the ship can be seen in the Ulster Folk and Transport Museum in Belfast.

unscrupulous ones to over-insure their ships in the hope of loss.

Modern ships have engines to get them out of trouble, radar, strong steel hulls, radio to report difficulties and weather forecasts to help them avoid them. Safety features are highly regulated. In theory and in practice they are many times safer than wooden sailing ships, but it also means that their owners expect much more from them, and sometimes push them too far. Arguably the *Titanic* was lost because of complacency about her safety and by taking her too close to icebergs in an attempt to beat the record for a transatlantic crossing. More recently, the car ferry *Herald of Free Enterprise* sank off Zeebrugge in 1987 because the bow doors were left open. Today, any shipwreck involving European or North American passengers or crew, or the spillage of oil or the death of sea birds, is highly publicised all round the world.

A shipwreck often causes large loss of life in dramatic circumstances, and gets full press attention. This tends to distort the fact that the sea is now a very safe way to travel.

The Lifeboat

Improvements in safety come in two ways – prevention of accidents, and means of rescue after they take place. For many centuries, sailors and landsmen alike accepted that sea travel was dangerous and nothing much could be done about it. By the end of the eighteenth century, certain philanthropists were beginning to think differently. In 1785 Lionel Lukin, a royal coachmaker, patented a boat with watertight compartments filled with cork to prevent it sinking. He was followed by Henry Greathead, a boatbuilder who witnessed the loss of a ship off South Shields in 1789 and built a 28-foot boat on the lines of a Greenland

Susan Ashley

THE main British collection of lifeboats is at the Historic Dockyard Chatham, where 17 are kept on behalf of the RNLI, including the *BASP* of 1924, the *St Cybi* of 1950, the *Grace Darling* of 1954, the *William and Fanny Kirby* of 1963 and the *Edward Bridges* of 1975.

The *Susan Ashley* was built by Groves and Gutteridge at Cowes in 1948 and was used at Sennen Cove in Cornwall until 1973. She is a twin-screw boat of the Watson type; she is 42 feet long. She was launched on service 87 times, saved 64 lives and helped to save five others. She also towed eight boats to safety.

LEFT
The *Susan Ashley* on display in one of the covered building slips at the Historic Dockyard Chatham.

whale boat with support from the Duke of Northumberland. The Admiralty tested it in 1808 and decided it would be too expensive to issue it to warships, but it was used in a few lifeboat stations round the coast.

The first great heroine of rescue was Grace Darling, the daughter of a lighthouse keeper in the Farne Islands off the coast of Northumberland. In 1838 she and her father saved nine people from the stricken steamer *Forfarshire* by rowing boat. The National Institution for the Preservation of Life from Shipwreck had been formed in 1824 and in 1854 it became the Royal National Lifeboat Institution (RNLI), to provide boats all round the British coast. It received a subsidy from the Board of Trade in its first 15 years, but apart from that it has relied entirely on charitable donations. The service was intended for lifesaving, not the more profitable salvage.

Early lifeboats were mostly designed for rowing, with auxiliary sail when conditions were right. Most were launched from beaches, some by hand, others drawn by horse. With differing conditions around the coast, there were local types such as the descendants of the Greathead boat in Northumberland, and the Norfolk and Suffolk further south. The first steam lifeboat, the *Duke of Northumberland*, was tested in 1891. Over time it became more common to launch lifeboats down a ramp, and the lifeboat

house became a feature of every seaside town. Other techniques, such as the development of the cork life jacket and the use of radio, made the service more efficient. The first motor lifeboats entered service in 1909. In 1963 the first inshore lifeboats were established. They were fast powerboats, which mostly helped yachtsmen, swimmers and other water sportsmen. Modern lifeboats are built in classes named after rivers, although the individual boats are often named after sponsors or lifeboat heroes. The large ones, such as the 52-foot Arun class, are kept afloat in harbour and crews board by dinghy.

The lifeboat service inspires more emotion than any other branch of maritime service, with its full share of heroes and disasters. Henry Blogg was perhaps the greatest hero. He began his 53 years of service with the Cromer lifeboat in 1894. Becoming coxswain in 1909, he saved 873 lives and was awarded the RNLI's gold medal three times, the last in 1941 when he rescued 88 men from ships in a convoy. He was also awarded the George Cross that year. One of the most emotive disasters was in March 1969. The lifeboat from Longhope in Orkney went to the rescue of a Liberian coaster and capsized with the loss of seven men including two families, each of a father and two sons.

As well as the lifeboat which could be launched from the shore, lifeboats borne by ships

could save lives in an emergency. Early ships invariably carried boats for many purposes, such as laying out anchors, transporting stores and ferrying officers and crew. They were not intended as lifeboats for they had no special measures to keep them afloat in dangerous weather and, in any case, could only carry about a quarter of the crew. Ships' lifeboats, with extra buoyancy, became common in the nineteenth century, although for a time regulation lagged behind the real possibilities of rescue. After the *Titanic* disaster, shipping line posters often stressed the number of lifeboats on the ship. Again they proved their value in two World Wars when thousands of seamen were saved after being torpedoed. But the Royal Navy's own lifesaving was inadequate for much of the wars, with a poorly designed inflatable lifejacket as standard.

Modern society tends to place much faith in lifeboats and rafts. Often it is very difficult to launch them all in bad conditions, or when the ship is listing. Inflatable life rafts are particularly difficult in strong winds, which can blow

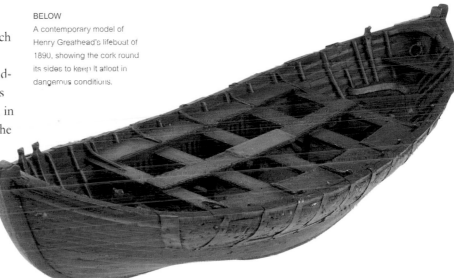

them away. One lesson of the Fastnet disaster of 1979 is not too take to liferafts too early – there were several cases where people abandoned yachts which survived the storm.

The Coastguard

HM Coastguard was founded in 1823 to guard the coast against smugglers, but it took on many other roles, such as reporting ship movements, changes in navigation marks and forming a reserve for the Royal Navy. In 1923 it was placed under the Board of Trade, with the main task of maritime safety, reporting shipwrecks and co-ordinating rescue efforts. It maintained stations around the coast, which kept a visual lookout until the 1970s, when radio and radar became predominant. It was responsible for enforcing traffic regulations in separations schemes, such as the first one in the Strait of Dover. It is one of the emergency services that can be reached by a 999 call. In 1998 it was merged with the Marine Safety Agency to form the Maritime and Coastguard Agency (MCA).

Safety at Sea

Although lifeboats could do much to rescue people, it was equally important to prevent accidents from happening. Collisions between sailing ships were not usually devastating but the introduction of steam in the early nineteenth century created new problems. Customs were already established regarding the precedence

ABOVE
The men of the Cornish village of
Cadgwith haul the new lifeboat
down rollers on the beach in 1947.
She was named *Guide of Dunkirk*
because of contributions by the
Girl Guides, and in memory of a
boat used at Dunkirk in 1940.

between sailing ships, for example the windward
one should give way. Subsequently, sail was
given precedence over steam, and new rules for
steamships were established. Ships were to steer
on the right in a narrow channel, and turn right
when meeting another head on. A ship should
give way to one approaching from its right, and
an overtaking vessel should keep clear of the
other ship until it was past and clear. But there
were still accidents. In 1878 the cargo ship
Bywell Castle sank the paddle steamer *Princess
Alice* in the Thames with the loss of 640 lives

including 126 children, mostly day-trippers
returning from Southend.

Samuel Plimsoll campaigned to have his
famous line marked on the sides of ships, to
show how deep it was allowed to float in certain circumstances, for example in Tropical
Fresh Water and in Winter North Atlantic.
This was enforced by law in 1876 and began
a period of parliamentary interest in maritime
safety. By the end of the century the condition
and conduct of merchant shipping was carefully regulated by British law, and this was emu-
lated by many other nations of the world. In
the second half of the twentieth century, bodies such as the International Maritime
Organisation, with its headquarters on the
south bank of the Thames, provide the regulations for world shipping.

Another approach was to improve the quali-
fications of the masters and mates of ships. In
1850 the Board of Trade began to examine can-
didates for certificates of competency as masters
and mates. These were eventually divided into
foreign-going certificates and home trade certificates, valid only in waters close to the United
Kingdom. Officers were compelled to keep logs
and observe safety precautions.

Lighthouses and Seamarks

Dangerous as it was, seafaring could always be
made easier and safer by marking some of the
hazards. The Romans were the first people to
built lighthouses in Britain, and one survives at

THE LOSS
OF THE
PRINCESS ALICE
SALOON STEAMER in the THAMES, Sept. 3rd, 1878.
AN AUTHENTIC NARRATIVE by a SURVIVOR, not hitherto published.
HEARTRENDING DETAILS—FACTS not MADE PUBLIC—NOBLE EFFORTS TO SAVE LIFE—ROBBING
THE DEAD—PARTICULARS AS TO LOST, SAVED, AND MISSING—PLAN OF THE LOCALITY.
SKETCHES BY AN EYE WITNESS.
BEAUTIFUL POEM, specially written on the event,
NOW FIRST PUBLISHED.
A MEMORIAL FOR ALL TIME OF THIS FEARFUL CALAMITY.
WHOLESALE OF J. F. NASH, 36, FLEET STREET, E.C.

RIGHT
A poster commemorating the
loss of the passenger steamer
Princess Alice in 1878, when
she was rammed by the larger
Bywell Castle.

Bell Rock Lighthouse

THE Bell Rock, 11 miles west of Arbroath in eastern Scotland, is perhaps the most dangerous hazard in British waters apart from Eddystone off Plymouth. It is on the main shipping route out of the Firths of Forth and Tay and along the North Sea coast. It is all the more dangerous, and difficult to build on, in that it is covered by 4 to 5 metres of water at high tide. According to legend the Abbot of Aberbrothock (Arbroath) put a bell on it to warn mariners in the fourteenth century. But the danger remained and it was believed that HMS *York* of 74 guns was lost on the rock with about 600 men in 1804.

Already Robert Stevenson, chief engineer to the Commissioners for the Northern Lights, was planning a lighthouse on the rock. In 1807 he set up his shore base at Arbroath, began cutting masonry and started to erect a wooden barrack on piles on the rock, working only at low tide. Work was suspended for the winter but began again in May 1808 when rocks were levelled off and three courses of masonry were completed before winter returned. The following year the structure was raised to 17 feet above high tide, and in 1810 it was complete, though it took some time to find red glass for the lantern and it was February 1811 before the lighthouse entered service. Even then there were disasters. The light was switched off in wartime unless specially requested and in 1915 the cruiser *Argyll* was lost, although the crew was saved.

The Bell Rock Lighthouse is naturally inaccessible, but the Signal Tower at Arbroath was the lighthouse's shore station. It has models and mementoes of the building of the lighthouse.

Dover Castle. Trinity House is responsible for navigation aids in the open seas around England and Wales, with the Commissioners for the Northern Lights assuming responsibility in Scotland. Many lighthouses were built round the coasts from the late eighteenth century onwards, to serve a dual purpose. As well as marking a danger, they give a navigator a recognisable point to take a bearing to help establish his position. Developments in light technology, notably the Fresnel lens of 1822 and the introduction of electric light, meant that signals are very reliable and can be projected over many miles. Each lighthouse has its own easily identifiable pattern of flashing light. Lightships also became common in English waters, where sandbanks are often the main danger. Since the 1980s all lighthouses and ships have been converted to automatic operation, serviced by helicopter. The lonely but rewarding trade of lighthouse keeper had become obsolete.

Local harbour authorities are in charge of the buoys and lights in their own areas, and it took some time before a universal system was applied. The British generally favoured flat-topped buoys to mark the port or left-hand side of a channel when entering harbour or with a rising tide, and pointed ones for the starboard side. The port-hand buoys were chequered red and black or white in England and Wales and black in Scotland, the starboard-hand ones were red or black. Selected buoys were lighted from the late nineteenth century, first with gas and then with electricity. In 1980 Britain adopted the International Association of Lighthouse Authorities (IALA) system with red for port hand and green for starboard. This also meant using the 'cardinal' system, which indicates safe water to the north, south, east or west of a hazard, and recognised marks for isolated dangers and safe water.

Chapter 13
Leisure and the Sea

Britain's island status provides a rich variety of maritime leisure experiences. It has numerous bathing beaches, which offer additional opportunities for surfing, windsurfing and kayaking. The long coastline has cliffs and rocks for walking and observing wildlife, and provides many harbours for yachts and sheltered water where faster sports such as water-skiing can take place. For the angler, whether inshore or on the sea, water is the last area open to the hunter-gatherer.

Britain has some of the best sailing areas in the world. The Solent is sheltered by the Isle of Wight and has both small and large harbours. It is near to London but also close enough to France for an overnight passage. The east coast offers a different kind of sailing, with sandbanks, small ports and the chance of a trip to Holland. The south-west of England, including the south coasts of Cornwall and Devon, is mainly about coastal sailing with spectacular scenery and historic harbours. In Scotland, the Firth of Clyde ranges from industrial towns on one side of the estuary, to the quiet of the Highlands on the other. The Crinan Canal gives easy access to the West Highlands and the islands of the Hebrides, where the scenery and the sailing experience more than compensate for the unreliable weather.

Charles II's Dutch Yachts

Even if leisure time was limited in past ages, people had known about the recreational possibilities of the sea for some time. A fifteenth-century manuscript in the British Library shows three people in a small boat partly covered with an awning, playing musical instruments and drinking from a jar. But a new word entered the English language in 1660, when the Dutch presented the newly restored Charles II with a *jacht*, which he called the *Mary*. Charles adapted the design to English standards and built a dozen yachts over the next 25 years, using them for military and diplomatic purposes, but also as personal pleasure craft. His brother James loved the sea equally well and the diarist John Evelyn records a race between them in 1661 for a wager of £100. They sailed down the Thames to Gravesend and back. 'The King lost it going, the wind being contrary, but saved stakes in returning'. Yachts were taken up by others on a grand or small scale. Lord Mordaunt built a vessel of more than 500 tons in 1681. Captain Jeremy Roch of the Royal Navy sailed from Plymouth to London and back in 1677 in an open sailing boat about 10 feet long. The following year he was in a much larger yacht, the *Mercury*, which was wrecked on the coast of Holland.

Early Yacht Clubs

Yachting was less central to the Hanoverian kings who ruled between 1714 and 1820, except for their annual visits to their other kingdom of Hanover. The constant wars also made yachting a precarious pursuit. But the public was very sea-minded, and in 1720 the first yacht club, the Water Club of Cork, was founded in the south of Ireland. Its members wore grand uniforms, and exercised like a fleet in pilot-cutter type vessels, but it had ended by 1765. The Cumberland Fleet, later the Royal Thames Yacht Club, was formed in 1775 and was sponsored by George III's uncle, the Duke of Cumberland. The Royal Yacht Squadron was founded soon after the great wars finished in 1815. It moved to Cowes on the Isle of Wight and became the most prestigious club in the world, and the only one entitled to fly the white ensign of the Royal Navy. By the late 1860s 33 clubs had been formed in Britain and Ireland.

Victorian Yachting

Nineteenth-century yachts usually had paid crews, and owners were advised on how to manage them. Paid masters should be 'alive to the serious responsibility of being in charge of a vessel'; those who were 'at one moment too familiar with the crew, at the next squabbling with them' were to be avoided. The crew should appear in 'the uniform of the yacht' in

Britannia

THE Royal Yacht *Britannia* was the last in a line going back to Queen Victoria's steamships and Charles II's sailing yachts. She was built at Clydebank and launched by Elizabeth II in 1953. She has three masts to carry a full complement of flags and her hull is painted royal blue. She was the only Royal Yacht to be designed for ocean cruising and had a speed of 21 knots. The royal compartments, including a verandah, dining room and drawing room, are aft of the engines. The crew of 271 was provided by the Royal Navy and lived forward of the engines. It was planned that the *Britannia* could be converted to a hospital ship in time of war, but this was not done during the Falklands Conflict of 1982.

The 3990-ton ship was very successful in projecting the image of the state during numerous royal visits over the 40 years following her launch, but already it was an old-fashioned one. Britain no longer had an Empire held together by sea power, and air was the main means of travel. The *Britannia* was used for the honeymoons of several ill-fated royal marriages – Princess Margaret and Anthony Armstrong-Jones in 1960, Prince Charles and

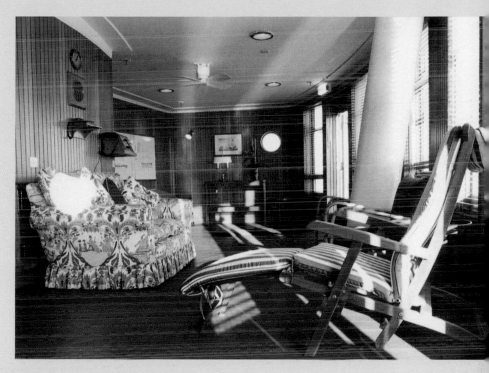

Lady Diana Spencer in 1981 and Prince Andrew and Sarah Ferguson in 1986. In 1997 she sailed from Hong Kong with Chris Patten, the departing governor of one of Britain's last colonies. She was taken out of service and became a tourist attraction in Leith docks, Edinburgh

ABOVE
The Royal Verandah near the stern of the *Britannia*.

daytime, although they could wear old clothes on night passages.

At the turn of the century a different style of yachting was emerging. In Erskine Childers' novel *Riddle of the Sands* (1903), Carruthers describes his arrival at his friend's yacht.

> Hazily there floated through my mind my last embarkation on a yacht; my faultless attire, the trim gig and obsequious sailors, the accommodation ladder flashing with varnish and brass in the August sun, the snowy decks with basket chairs under the awning aft. What a contrast with this sordid midnight scramble, over damp meat and littered packing cases!

Royal Yachts

Queen Victoria was not perhaps a natural seafarer, even if she did put several of her sons into the navy. She took advantage of the new age of the steamship, and royal yachts carried her around her kingdom. Her favourite home was at Osborne on the Isle of Wight, and she used a succession of small paddle steamers to take her there from Portsmouth Dockyard.

Queen Victoria had three yachts in succession named *Victoria and Albert*. The last one was built in 1899 and remained afloat for more than 50 years until she was replaced by the *Britannia* in 1953.

Steam Yachts

Steam yachting began with Thomas Assheton-Smith, who left the Royal Yacht Club in 1830. But the steam engine of the time was noisy, expensive and took up a good deal of space so only three steam yachts were registered in 1850. The compound engine was slightly more suitable, but 40 per cent of space on a boat might still have to be allocated for the engine. There were 384 steam yachts on the register by 1882, 275 of them under 100 tons, and only 12 of them over 500 tons.

Petrol and diesel engines became more common in the early years of the twentieth century

and smaller boats known as cabin cruisers were built, either to sail the seas in good weather, or for family cruises on rivers and canals. Powerboat races were developed from the early twentieth century and became popular in the 1920s and 1930s. By the 1930s many sailing yachts had small engines, especially after the outboard motor was developed; but the sailing yacht would survive much better than other types of vessel.

Holiday Resorts

Early in the eighteenth century wealthy Englishmen began to discover the virtues of sea bathing in preserving health, and the resort of Scarborough began to compete with inland spas such as Harrogate. In 1753 Dr Richard Russell published a treatise on the beneficial effects of sea water and the southern resort of Brighton began to develop. Early in the nineteenth century the seaside resorts were opened up to larger numbers of people by the steamship, and piers were built to cater for passengers. In the English resorts rail travel became more important from

the 1840s onwards, and the piers were adapted to be used as entertainment arcades. The resorts of the Firth of Clyde in Scotland were less accessible by land and the piers have remained in use for transport in Rothesay and Dunoon to the present day.

The resorts became ever more popular by the end of the nineteenth century, with day and weekend excursions for those who could not afford a full holiday. The seaside developed distinctive architecture, with extravagant styles such as the Royal Pavilion at Brighton, great dignity in many ranges of Georgian buildings, rows of houses converted to bed and breakfast hotels and gaudy theatres and arcades. Every form of entertainment was available but the beach remained the centrepiece of the resort, with donkey rides, Punch and Judy shows, deck chairs and ice-cream sellers.

Resorts continued to boom in the twentieth century despite the interruptions of the wars. Paid holidays became normal in the 1930s, causing Billy Butlin to set up his first holiday camps. Caravan sites filled many of the vacant

ABOVE

The Palace Pier at Brighton was built between 1891 and 1899 and plays host to 2 million visitors a year. It is 1722 feet long and its attractions include a funfair, bars, rides, restaurants and fortune-tellers.

Blackpool Seaside Resort

WITH several miles of beaches and within easy reach of the industrial cities in Lancashire and Yorkshire, the resort of Blackpool began to emerge in the eighteenth century and had four hotels by 1780. It developed far more rapidly in the next century, particularly with the coming of the railway, with the population increasing a hundredfold to more than 47,000 by 1901. The North Pier was built in 1863, the Central Pier in 1868 and the South Pier in 1804. Blackpool's most famous feature, the Tower, which opened in the same year, was modelled on the Eiffel Tower in Paris.

Blackpool was the first town to use electric street lighting in 1879, and in 1912 it introduced its famous Illuminations, which are held in the autumn to extend the holiday season by a further eight weeks. Today Blackpool is as popular as ever, offering leisure parks and nightclubs along its 12 miles of Promenade. The town's famous trams carry about 120,000 visitors along the Promenade on a busy summer's day.

Blackpool Tower and the sea front during the Illuminations in the autumn.

spaces along the coast in the 1950s. But cheap flights to Spain and rising living standards hit the British beaches hard in the 1960s. They survived and still offer a leisure experience that is close to home for most Britons.

The Cruise Industry

Cruising was invented in 1835 when Arthur Anderson, later to found P&O, advertised for an imaginary cruise to the Faroe Islands and Iceland – apparently to fill up space in a newspaper he published in Shetland. The idea caught on. His company made more practical voyages, also to the north, in the late 1880s when two ships cruised round Norwegian waters, and Mediterranean cruises began soon afterwards. Cruising boomed in the 1960s, as the redundant Atlantic liners sought a new market. The economic boom provided the customers, while the airliner, which had driven the liner out of business, allowed passengers to be flown anywhere in the world to join their ship

– thereby avoiding the most turbulent sea conditions experienced rounding Cape Horn and the Cape of Good Hope.

Cruising is now aimed at those of moderate means rather than the very rich, though it retains its opulent image. The British provide hundreds of thousands of cruise passengers every year, although they are a long way behind America, which provides millions. Cruise ships do sail in British waters and Southampton has a large terminal, but they are less popular than those in the Mediterranean and the Caribbean, where the weather is more reliable. The main British cruise company is P&O, which operates four main ships. The *Oceania* of 77,000 tons has room for more than 2000 passengers in 1000 cabins. Their subsidiary, Swan Hellenic, specialises in study cruises mainly in the Mediterranean. Cunard is another large player. The *Queen Elizabeth 2* was converted from the Atlantic liner service and their *Queen Mary 2* of 2004 has room for 2620 passengers.

The Leisure Boom

The economic boom from the 1950s onwards increased most people's wealth and reduced working hours, bringing yachting of one form or another within reach of the great majority of the population. New materials made boats cheaper, electronics made navigation easier, and there was a strong desire to escape from the confined environment of the cities. Today, water sports are enormously popular, putting great pressure on space in busy yachting areas such as the south of England. More than 16,000 boats were based in 14 harbours in the Solent area in 1974, rising to nearly 28,000 by 1989.

After the Second World War fibreglass was used for moulding the hulls of yachts and powerboats, allowing mass production for the first time. Multihull shapes, such as the catamaran, give much greater speed, but are more demanding to sail. Most sailing yachts carry a diesel or petrol engine, for it is virtually impossible to manoeuvre in a modern marina under sail. Masts are usually made of aluminium for strength and lightness, and sails of artificial materials such as Terylene. Ropes are made of wire, Nylon or Polypropylene. A Global Positioning System (GPS) has a continuous read-out allowing an exact position to be plotted on a chart, but yachtsmen are still encouraged to learn traditional navigation, to know what to do in the event of electronic failure.

Many thousands of yachts take part in local regattas, or cruise round the coast from port to port. The best-known type is the sailing cruiser, usually from 18 to 45 feet long with accommodation on board, of varying standards of comfort. Most have a single mast with one

BELOW
A model of the cruise ship *Grand Princess*, built for P&O in Italy in 1999 to carry 2600 passengers. Seventy per cent of her passenger cabins have a sea view.

Gipsy Moth IV

FRANCIS Chichester had set many aviation records in the 1930s before he took up long-distance sailing. He won the first single-handed transatlantic race in his boat *Gipsy Moth II* in 1960. *Gipsy Moth IV* was built by Camper and Nicholson at Southampton in 1965 and is 54 feet long, with a two-masted ketch rig. Chichester described her as 'about as unbalanced and unstable a boat there could be', but he made a single-handed round-the-world voyage at the age of 65 between August 1966 and May 1967. One of his chief aims was to equal the average passage time of the wool clipper ships to Australia via the Cape of Good Hope. He took 107 days to reach Sydney, 20 days faster than the average time of all the clippers. He spent 48 days re-fitting and re-provisioning in Sydney before setting off for home via Cape Horn. He was knighted with Drake's sword at Greenwich soon after his return. *Gipsy Moth IV* was put on display near the *Cutty Sark* at Greenwich until she was taken away in 2004, to be restored for further round-the-world voyages.

LEFT
Gipsy Moth IV off Greenwich in August 1966 before her round-the-world voyage, with the *Cutty Sark* in the background.

triangular sail, the headsail, forward of the mast and one, the mainsail, aft of it. Most sailing cruisers have a fin-shaped ballast keel about 1.5–2 metres into the water to improve the yacht's stability in heavy weather and rough seas.

The sailing dinghy is a small open boat with a light and retractable keel. The crew often has to lean over the side to stop the boat capsizing in strong winds; even so, a dinghy sailor must be ready to fall in the water from time to time. Some dinghies are of 'one-design' classes used by local clubs for their own conditions. Others are mass produced in fibreglass and wood. The most popular was the *Mirror*, sponsored by the newspaper of that name. It was designed by the yachting guru, Uffa Fox, and Barry Bucknell, presenter of Britain's first do it-yourself television programme, in the 1950s. More than 47,000 had been built by 1975.

Epic Voyages

Many millions follow the activities of sailing heroes and heroines, mostly in single-handed long-distance voyages or races. They were not voyages of discovery in the old sense, but they show human endurance at its limits. One of the first single-handed sailors was John MacGregor, who built his canoe *Rob Roy* in 1865. He sailed down the Rhine, Danube and Seine, toured Norway, Sweden and Denmark and canoed through the Suez Canal and down the Red Sea. Francis Chichester made a single-handed one-stop round-the-world voyage in *Gipsy Moth IV*. Robin Knox-Johnson was the first to sail the world nonstop in his ketch *Suhaili* in 1968–9, in 313 days from Falmouth, England and back again. Chay Blyth sailed against the prevailing winds in his ketch *British Steel* in 1970–71.

Ellen MacArthur first sprang to fame in 2001 when, at the age of 24, she came second in the Vendee Globe round-the-world race. In February 2005, amid great popular excitement, she completed another round-the-world passage and reduced the world record time by more than a day to 71 days, 14 hours and 18 minutes.

New Sports

The surfboard has become popular on the Atlantic coast of Cornwall, where impressive waves break on to the beaches. Its descendant, the sail board or windsurfer, has also become a common pastime.

British canoeists mostly use a variant of the Inuit Kayak rather than the North American Indian canoe. They are an exciting means of venturing up rivers that are not otherwise navigable, and are also used on the open sea and in races on flat water. British waters offer many opportunities for scuba diving, particularly off the south and west coasts.

Inland Waterways

British canals and river transport continued to decline in the 1950s in competition with road transport, and many waterways were allowed to fall into decay. But already waterway holidays of different types were becoming popular. They need less skill than navigation on the seas and there is no risk of seasickness. Most canals are only navigable by the traditional narrow boat, because their locks are so small. Speed is restricted to 4 miles an hour and there are many locks, so progress is slow but relaxing. The Norfolk Broads offer a variety of holidays with both sailing and power boats, few locks, rivers and small lakes. Rivers, such as the Thames above London, are navigable without much skill and allow the traveller to enter a

completely different world only a few miles from the centre of the city.

The leisure use of waterways caused a considerable revival. The Kennet and Avon Canal crosses southern England between Reading and Bath and was re-opened in 1990. It includes the famous Caen Hill flight of 17 locks. The Forth and Clyde Canal across central Scotland was also restored and the Falkirk Wheel was built to raise boats from one level to another. Meanwhile the network of canals linking the towns of the industrial English Midlands and North continued in service. There are 4000 miles of navigable waterways in Britain, half of them canals administered by the British Waterways Board.

ABOVE
Locks at Foxton on the Grand Union Canal near Market Harborough. Built in 1810, the series of 10 raises a boat by 22.5 metres.

Rowing

Rowing regattas are recorded as early as 1775, and the famous Boat Race between Oxford and Cambridge began on the River Thames in 1829. A special type of boat evolved, with no keel, sliding seats and outriggers for the oars. The Henley Regatta began further up the Thames in 1839 and became Royal in 1851. It is the great national and international event of the sport. Rowing is also popular on other rivers such as the Severn. Another kind of rowing takes place off the coasts of south-west England. Local pilot gigs are narrow, fast clinker-built craft and each coastal town has its own crew who take part in annual races.

Yacht Races

Yacht racing became popular in the nineteenth century. The United States schooner *America* beat all comers round the Isle of Wight in 1851 and since then the Americas Cup has been widely seen as sailing's most prestigious race. British teams have tried to win the cup back, often supported by wealthy businessmen such as Sir Thomas Lipton, but they have always failed.

At the other end of the scale, small boat, or 'dinghy' racing originated in the second half of the nineteenth century. The Suffolk 'Model'

Yacht Club was founded in 1864 and five years later its members had a dozen boats, mostly 14-foot cutters for racing. Many yacht clubs produced classes suitable for local conditions. Two schools developed in England, one in the West Country port of Teignmouth, the other in the inland waterways of Norfolk. In 1911 a race between the two types was won by the West Country vessel.

In 1875 the Yacht Racing Association, now the Royal Yachting Association or RYA, was formed to provide uniform rules. Boats were originally divided into six classes, ranging from under 3 tons to over 80 tons. Designers soon began 'building to the rules', interpreting them to the best advantage, so they had to be changed constantly to close loopholes. The 1920s and 1930s were generally an age of smaller boats owned by the rising middle classes. The naval architect, Uffa Fox, designed boats with V-shaped bottoms and these became standard for racing dinghies. At the other end of the scale were the great yachts of the J class, which competed for the Americas Cup and other races. The most famous yacht of the age was the cutter *Britannia*, built for the Prince of Wales (later Edward VII) in 1893 and scuttled on the death of George V in 1935.

BELOW
Yachts racing off the Isle of Wight during Cowes Week. The brightly coloured, balloon-like sails are spinnakers

Other internationally known races in British waters include the Fastnet Race from the English coast around the Fastnet Rock and its lighthouse off the south coast of Ireland and back again. The Admiral's Cup, organised by the Royal Ocean Racing Club and first held in 1957, is a series of races between national teams. The Whitbread round-the-world race, now the Volvo Ocean Race, began in 1973, and the first *Observer* transatlantic race, between Plymouth and Newport on Rhode Island, was held in 1981. At a much more modest level, yacht races are held by nearly all local clubs. Dinghies are used mainly for racing and training, with a minority preferring to use them for cruising.

British teams have always been highly successful in Olympic competitions. This was particularly true in 2004, when Shirley Robertson's team won the country's first gold medal of the games,

in the Yngling class. Combined with Ben Ainslie's gold in the Finn class and Matthew Pinsent's crew in rowing, as well as success in Kayak and three other sailing classes, including the first-ever windsurfing place, Britain won more medals on the water than any other nation.

Sail Training and Tall Ships Races

Britain has surprisingly few 'tall ships' left in the popular sense of the term. The only square-rigged ship that has operated consistently in British waters since the 1970s is the brig *Royalist*, which looks tiny alongside the German ships which were distributed among the former allies at the end of the Second World War, for example the Russian *Krushenstern*. Nevertheless, Britain originated the Tall Ships Races in 1956. They have been largely run by the Sail Training Association since then and

BELOW
The *Sir Winston Churchill* was built for the Sail Training Association in 1966 for the training of young people. She made her final journey in December 2000. All her sails are set in this picture, but it is difficult to keep them all filled with wind.

most of the annual races include a visit to a British port. In fact the official definition of 'tall ship' includes many small, fore-and-aft rigged vessels so the British entry to the races is quite respectable.

Sailing Schools

The sailing yacht requires a greater range of skills than any other leisure activity. The RYA provides theoretical and practical training at a variety of levels from 'Competent Crew' to 'Yachtmaster Ocean', able to take charge of a yacht in any circumstances. This is voluntary in Britain, as the RYA campaigns to keep boating free of compulsory registration.

Marinas

Marinas are purpose-built yacht harbours. The boats are moored to floating pontoons, which rise and fall with the tide. Each is a narrow 'finger' allowing the maximum number of boats in a given space. Some marinas, such as Brighton, are created artificially by excavating the land or building breakwaters. Most marinas have a full range of facilities for yachts including repair, sales, charter and clubs.

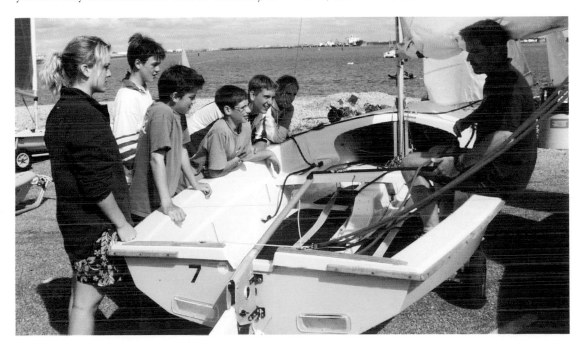

Chapter 14
The World Wars

The Start of the Naval War

Britain entered the First World War on 4 August 1914, as Germany invaded Belgium as a way of outflanking the French defences. Russia was also an ally against the Central Powers of Germany and Austria-Hungary. The fleet was quickly mobilised under Winston Churchill as First Lord of the Admiralty, but there was embarrassment in the Mediterranean when two German ships, the *Goeben* and *Breslau,* escaped and were given to Turkey, causing that country to enter the war on the German side. Italy joined the Allies in 1915, so the Mediterranean was largely under Allied control.

One of the greatest British fears was German surface ships raiding the lines of communication. Early in November 1914 a German squadron under Admiral Graf Spee defeated a smaller British one at Coronel off the coast of Chile. Reinforcements were sent out, including the battle cruiser *Invincible*, and the German force was destroyed near the Falkland Islands. Other raiders, such as the *Karlsruhe* and *Emden* were hunted down.

Meanwhile a great force of Dreadnought battleships, supported by cruisers and destroyers, was constituted into the Grand Fleet under Admiral Jellicoe. It took up its base at Scapa Flow in Orkney, but soon had to leave it temporarily for fear of submarine attack. The Battle Cruiser Fleet under Admiral Beatty was based further south in the Firth of Forth. Though it would link up with the Grand Fleet in battle to serve as a reconnaissance and striking force, it was largely independent of it, and was by far the most publicised part of the navy.

But the great naval battle predicted by experts did not materialise. The Germans knew that they were numerically inferior, by about three to two. They had no reason to risk a battle between the two fleets. The British patrolled the North Sea, the Germans bombarded coastal towns such as Great Yarmouth and Hartlepool, hoping to lure out small British squadrons. There was a skirmish at Heligoland Bight in August 1914, and a larger battle at Dogger Bank in January 1915. Beatty's battle cruisers caught a German squadron, but failed to destroy it due to signalling errors. The land war settled into bloody stalemate on the Western Front. The sea was equally static, far less bloody but deeply disappointing for the navy.

Jutland and its Aftermath

Both the Battle Cruiser Fleet and the Grand Fleet left harbour in the evening of 30 May 1916, intending to link up off the coast of Denmark. The German High Seas Fleet under Admiral Scheer had also left port, and Beatty's battle cruisers made contact with its scouting force at 4 p.m. the next day. The Germans drew Beatty's ships south on to the guns of their main fleet, and Beatty lost two of his battle cruisers due to explosions in the magazines. The Fifth Battle Squadron, attached to the battle cruisers, contained the most powerful battleships in the world but was late in entering the action due to signalling error and lack of initiative.

Beatty drew the Germans north where Jellicoe deployed the Grand Fleet of 24 battleships into a single line, ready to 'cross the T' of the enemy, to deploy the maximum amount of gun power on his leading ships. Scheer quickly turned away to evade this. He was now cut off from his bases and turned eastwards, only to have his T crossed again. This time he launched an attack by torpedo boats, which forced Jellicoe, cautious as ever, to turn away himself. The main fleets lost contact. There were several desultory night actions with destroyers and cruisers, but the High Seas Fleet succeeded in escaping to its bases. In all, the British lost three battle cruisers and 11 other ships with 6000 men; the Germans lost one battle cruiser and a pre-Dreadnought battleship with nine other ships and 2500 men. They were quick to claim the victory, and the British were disconcerted that it was very far from a second Trafalgar. But the High Seas Fleet had retreated, and in effect it had given up any hope of defeating the Grand Fleet.

As a result of Jutland, Jellicoe was 'kicked upstairs' to become First Sea Lord and professional head of the navy, and Beatty took command of the Grand Fleet. There were no further battles and life at Scapa Flow slipped further into tedium. It did, however, give the navy time to

The beach at Courseulles in Normandy soon after D-Day, by Stephen Bone. Amphibious craft known as DUKWs are landing stores from ships offshore. In the foreground is an army and navy beach party, which controls the traffic in the area.

300,000 allied troops from the beaches and harbour of Dunkirk, mostly by regular war-ships and passenger vessels, but with the help of small boats and motor yachts, which ferried men from the beaches to the larger ships.

The nation now prepared to defend itself against a German invasion. Destroyers and cruis-ers were moved south but the battleships remained in Scapa Flow where they were safer from enemy attack. If the RAF had failed to save the country in the Battle of Britain in the summer of 1940, the navy would have been called upon to smash the invasion force, but it never sailed.

Churchill was determined not to sink into a purely defensive mentality, and founded Combined Operations immediately after Dunkirk to plan a re-invasion of the continent, and to mount regular raids with new troops known as commandos, who would be landed by ship or submarine. Coastal warfare devel-oped in the English Channel and North Sea, although the German fast craft, known in Britain as E-boats, were larger and superior to their British equivalents, the Motor Torpedo

Boats and Motor Gunboats. Control of the Channel remained under dispute. Partly due to lack of co-operation with the RAF, the German battle cruisers *Scharnhorst* and *Gneisenau* were able to pass through the Strait of Dover with-out damage in February 1942.

The War in the Mediterranean

With the entry of Italy to the war in June 1940 and the loss of France, the British were drawn into a war in the Mediterranean and North Africa. The first task was the unpleasant one of disposing of the French fleets at Mers el Kebir, so that it could not be adopted into the German navy. The Mediterranean Fleet was successful in several actions against the Italians. Torpedo bombers sank several major ships in harbour at Taranto in 1940, reversing the old belief that a fleet was safe in harbour and giving the Japanese some lessons for Pearl Harbour the following year. At Matapan in March 1941, they fought a surface action with the Italians and sank three cruisers. But the British suffered from lack of air cover themselves, especially against German dive

HMS *Cavalier*

HMS *Cavalier* was launched in the Isle of Wight shipyard of J and S White in April 1944, one of the last of the War Emergency programme of 96 destroyers. Commissioned in the November, she was armed with four 4.5-inch guns in single turrets, eight torpedo tubes and anti aircraft guns. Her 40,000-horsepower engines drove her at more than 36 knots and the standard crew for her class was 186 to 222 officers and men. She was 339 feet 6 inches long and displaced 1710 tons.

Despite her late entry, the *Cavalier* saw some action in the Second World War, taking part in three operations off Norway and acting in defence of the Russian convoy RA64. She then found time to take part in the bombardment of Surabaja, Java, before the Pacific War ended. She was modernised in 1955–7 and fitted with anti-submarine mortars and the latest anti-aircraft guns and equipment. In 1962 she helped defend the Sultan of Brunei against a rebellion and in 1964 she was refitted again, with the Seacat guided missile. In 1970 she helped rescue the Scottish coaster *St Brandan* and the following year she raced HMS *Rapid* over a 64-mile course to win the title of the 'fastest ship in the fleet'. In 1972 she was sold by the Royal Navy and attempts were made to preserve her as the last of the wartime destroyers. She was moved to Southampton, Brighton and Tyneside before finding a permanent home at Chatham Historic Dockyard in 1999.

bombers. Their resources were diverted by the need to defend Malta and to keep that island supplied by sending several convoys, which suffered heavy losses. However, submarines based in Malta took a heavy toll of enemy shipping and had a decisive effect on the campaign in North Africa. An intervention in defence of Greece failed when German troops began to support the Italians and the navy withdrew British forces. The Germans invaded Crete by air in May 1941 and British troops had to be withdrawn yet again. The navy suffered some of its heaviest losses of the war, but 17,000 men were taken off. Later in the year the Mediterranean Fleet reached it lowest point when the battleship *Barham* was sunk by U-boat and two more battleships were severely damaged by Italian midget submarines in Alexandria Harbour.

The Malta convoys of 1942, including Pedestal in August, were the hardest fought of all and barely succeeded in keeping the island in the war at the cost of heavy naval losses. But American resources were coming into play and the land war took a turn for the better after the Battle of El Alamein in October. In November British and US forces landed in French North Africa and the Germans and Italians were driven out by an advance from both ends. In July 1943 the Allies launched a successful amphibious invasion of Sicily, followed by landings in Italy. It was not the 'soft underbelly of Europe' that Churchill had hoped and the armies were soon bogged down against German resistance. Italy was knocked out of the war and her fleet surrendered, giving the Allies control of the Mediterranean.

The Personnel of the Navy

In the First World War the navy had relied largely on its existing reserves and on civilians brought into the RNAS and the Patrol Service. In the Second it had to expand to a much greater extent, and more than a million men and women served in it between 1939 and 1945. It had to acquire skills in training raw conscripts to become sailors. It developed the Fleet Air Arm from almost nothing and took on new technology such as radar. It had to build up a huge number of landing ships and craft for the re-invasion of Europe and train crews for them. It extended the idea of using women in shore jobs. In the past they had served as cooks and clerks, but now they were trained as signallers and mechanics as well. All this was done within a very traditional framework, in which old naval values and customs were used to establish morale.

At the top the navy was blessed with a number of great admirals and captains, with far more initiative than their predecessors in the last war. Andrew Cunningham commanded the Mediterranean Fleet through its most difficult years and gained a reputation as the greatest British sailor since Nelson. Max Horton directed the Battle of the Atlantic and Bertram Ramsay organised the Dunkirk evacuation and, with perfect symmetry, commanded the naval forces during the Normandy invasion of 1944. There were great fleet commanders such as Sir Bruce Fraser and Sir Philip Vian, and submarine captains such as David Wanklyn and Anthony Miers.

The Battle of the Atlantic

Having failed to invade Britain or subdue the country by bombing in the winter of 1940–41, the Germans now had only the U-boat to secure her objective. As Churchill proclaimed in March 1941, 'The Battle of the Atlantic has now begun'. Battle was something of an understatement for a campaign that was to last for the rest of the war and involve the navies of Britain, Canada and the USA, the merchant fleets of these and many other countries, as well as scientists, shipbuilders, dockers and, not least, the intelligence services. The submarine campaign had already proved effective and the U-boat commanders enjoyed a 'happy time' in the winter of 1940–41. British resources were inadequate to protect the lifeline across the Atlantic. Modern warships had to be withdrawn for home defence. The newly built escort vessels, the corvettes, had been designed for coastal rather than ocean duties but had to be used as nothing else was available. Fifty old destroyers from the neutral USA were no better as sea boats.

In May 1941 the powerful German battleship *Bismarck* sailed into the Atlantic. She sank the battle cruiser *Hood*, the pride of the Royal Navy, but was damaged by attacks from carrier-borne Swordfish aircraft and her steering put out of action. She was tracked down and destroyed by the British Fleet.

By the spring of 1941 the U-boat position improved and the British were increasingly able to use Ultra to decode German radio messages in the Enigma code, thus giving warning of attack. But the US entry to the war after Pearl Harbour in December did not help in the Atlantic. Most ships were withdrawn to the Pacific and there was no convoy system on the American east coast. The U-boats enjoyed

another 'happy time' for the first half of 1942 when they sank thousands of tons of shipping in sight of America.

After that the U-boats returned to mid-Atlantic and the Battle reached a climax in the spring of 1943. Two convoys, HX 229 and SC 122, were heavily attacked in March. Fortunately help was on the way. New weapons such as hedgehog, an ahead firing mortar, which removed some of the disadvantages of depth charges, entered service. The RAF was at last prevailed upon to provide enough aircraft and training for long-range reconnaissance. The supply of escorts improved with ships built in the USA and the new British frigates, and it was possible to form support groups to come to the aid of beleaguered convoys. Radar was increasingly used to detect U-boats on the surface. In May, convoy ONS 5 forced its way through the greatest concentration of U-boats so far, with acceptable losses and with some damage to the enemy. Karl Dönitz, the German commander, was forced to withdraw his boats from the Atlantic.

ABOVE

The mulberry harbour at Arromanches in Normandy in June 1944 showing the concrete breakwaters with the floating piers behind, by Stephen Bone.

It was not the end of the U-boat war. In 1944 the Germans developed the *schnorkel*, which allowed them to remain underwater for much longer periods, and began a campaign in British inshore waters. But it was too late; victory in the Atlantic had already allowed the Allies to build up huge military forces in Britain, supported by the tanks, aircraft, fuel and stores needed for the next venture.

D-Day and the Invasion of Europe

Since Dunkirk the British had planned meticulously for their return to the continent, setting up a new organisation and developing many ships and craft to achieve this. The problem was far more difficult than in previous wars, for an invading army would need to take tanks, vehicles and fuel with it and to have constant communication with supporting air power. A disastrous raid on Dieppe in 1942 provided some lessons, as did the invasion in the Mediterranean.

When the Allies invaded Normandy on 6 June 1944, the Royal Navy provided about half the landing vessels. These included landing ships which could undertake ocean voyages and launch landing craft on to the beaches; tank landing craft which could carry vehicles over the whole route; craft carrying guns and rockets which could go far inshore and engage with the enemy on land; kitchen boats to keep the troops

and sailors fed; and headquarters ships with all the radar and radio necessary to control a battle on land, sea and air. The Royal Navy also provided about three-quarters of the supporting ships, including battleships and cruisers to give gun support, destroyers and frigates to keep away enemy U-boats and destroyers, and midget submarines and coastal craft to guide the landing force to its destination. Artificial harbours known as mulberries were transported across the Channel, and a pipeline known as Pluto was planned to supply oil, although it was less successful than had been hoped.

The Royal Navy figures less in the standard histories than it deserves, mainly because it made the invasion on the British and Canadian beaches look too easy. It took place with minimum casualties, though the weather was far from ideal. The land campaign, however, soon became bogged down. The navies spent the next few months keeping the armies supplied by sea until the German surrender in May 1945.

The War in the Far East

As war with Japan threatened in 1941, Churchill sent the capital ships *Prince of Wales* and *Repulse* to the region. This did nothing to deter the attack on the US base at Pearl Harbour on 7 December 1941, and the two ships themselves were lost three days later to

HMS *Belfast*

HMS *Belfast* was begun at the end of 1936 in the Harland and Wolff shipyard in the city after which she was named. Designed partly in response to the Japanese *Mogami* class, with her sister-ship *Edinburgh* she was one of the largest British cruisers, at 10,000 tons, and with a main armament of twelve 6-inch guns in four turrets. She was commissioned a month before the outbreak of war in 1939, and on 21 November she was the first major casualty of the German magnetic mine in the Firth of Forth. She spent nearly three years under repair at Devonport, during which she was enlarged and fitted with the latest equipment such as radar. She joined the Home Fleet at Scapa Flow, mostly escorting convoys to Russia, and in December 1943 she took part in the sinking of the German *Scharnhorst* off Norway, the Royal Navy's last major gun action. She covered the Fleet Air Arm's strike against the battleship *Tirpitz* in 1944 and bombarded the Normandy coast during the landings of 6 June. After that she was refitted for service in the Far East but the war ended before she got there. She helped to cover the escape of HMS *Amethyst* from the Chinese Communists in 1949 and the following year she began service in the Korean War, during which she patrolled the west coast of the country. She saw much service in the Far East in the next decade but by 1971 she was one of the few cruisers left in the Royal Navy. She was paid off in that year and put into the care of the Imperial War Museum. She is now afloat in the Thames opposite the Tower of London, the largest surviving British warship from either World War. She shows much detail of life on board a warship in the mid twentieth century.

BELOW
HMS *Belfast* moored in central London. The camouflage scheme dates from the Second World War.

Japanese bombers, Churchill's delight at US entry to the war soon turned to despair as Hong Kong and Singapore were taken by the Japanese in the most humiliating moment of the British Empire. Light British forces remained in the Indian Ocean, but the Pacific War was an American concern and they deployed huge resources to it. They developed aircraft carrier task forces, which were far beyond British means, and used aircraft that outclassed the British ones. As the naval war with Germany began to wind down, the British Pacific Fleet was formed in 1944 and sent east. It was far outnumbered by the Americans, and had not yet developed the techniques of replenishment at sea that gave the Americans tactical mobility on a broad ocean. The British sailors were war-weary and had far less of a personal interest in the Pacific than the Americans. They were beginning to notice that American pay and conditions were far superior by the time the atom bomb ended the war in August 1945.

Chapter 15
Maritime Art

For at least four centuries, the sea has provided Britons with the inspiration for some of the greatest works of art. The sea itself, with its varied colours, its changing moods, its perspective over the ocean and its crashing waves, has been painted by generations of artists. Looking to the shore, the coastlines provide a variety of landscape and sometimes a geological cross section exposing the strata of past ages. The sea is also the passageway to many different worlds and it inspires tales of shipwreck, exploration, piracy and naval warfare. The ship is an enclosed and very intense world to use as a setting for stories. And a seafaring nation naturally picks up culture from all around the world and incorporates it within its own.

Paintings and Drawings

Maritime societies do not necessarily produce great maritime art – the Venetians ruled the seas in the fifteenth century and had many great painters such as the Bellinis and Titian, but left very few paintings of the sea. The first real maritime artists were the Dutch during their golden age in the sixteenth and seventeenth centuries. The greatest of all were the Van de Veldes, father and son, who drew and painted sea battles and merchant ships before being attracted to the rising sea power of England in 1673. As well as recording the ships and activities of Charles II's navy, they gave a boost to British marine art. The generation that followed the death of the

younger Van de Velde in 1707 had the elements of a native English style but was rather inferior. The middle of the eighteenth century saw the short career of Charles Brooking, who died at the age of 36 in 1759. His profound understanding of ships in the sea is reflected in a small number of very fine paintings. John Cleveley the Elder (1712–77) produced very accurate paintings of ships in the Royal Dockyards, particularly Deptford, but there is no sign he ever went to sea. Nicolas Pocock, on the other hand, had been a sea captain and made beautifully illustrated logbooks of his voyages to the West Indies before setting up as a marine painter at the age of 39 in 1780. He painted many sea battles including Copenhagen and Trafalgar and was present at St Vincent. The new generation of marine artists had no trouble finding patrons among wealthy naval captains, businesses and charitable societies, and for book illustrations.

The early nineteenth century saw the flourishing of J M W Turner, the giant of British painting. A large number of his works had a maritime theme, including numerous views of harbours and coasts, a rather inaccurate painting of Trafalgar and one of his most famous, *The Fighting Temeraire*, depicting the old sailing warship being towed to the scrap yard by a steam tug. His contemporary, E W Cooke, was a child prodigy, who published his plates of *Shipping and Craft* at the age of 17 in 1828. He had a long career and travelled extensively in

ABOVE

Ships in a Light Breeze by Charles Brooking, who died at the age of 36. The art historian David Cordingly writes of his 'ability to fill a painting with a breeze – a breeze which whips up waves, tightens ropes, puffs out sails and heels over ships and small boats'.

Europe. James McNeill Whistler (1834–1903) painted many views of the sea and the River Thames, but by the late nineteenth century the most prominent artists were taking less interest in marine painting. There was still plenty of commissions, however, for book illustrations and paintings to hang in boardrooms. The most prolific marine artist of the period was William L Wyllie, who had a long career until his death at 80 in 1931. He created many pictures of barges on the Rivers Thames and Medway, drawings of warships, including the Grand Fleet in the First World War, and a famous panorama of Trafalgar. Today marine painting flourishes, although it is far from the mainstream of art. Book covers provide a major source of support, including the paintings by Geoff Hunt RSMA for the Patrick O'Brian novels and other works.

The Sea in Literature

The earliest English playwrights, including William Shakespeare, made numerous references to the sea, although nearly always offstage. *The Tempest* is written around the effects of a shipwreck, the plot of *The Merchant of Venice* hinges on the loss of Antonio's ships, including

one on the Goodwin Sands, 'a very dangerous flat and fatal, where the carcasses of many a tall ship lie buried'. The wars with France produced plays such as *The Fair Quaker of Deal*, written in 1710 and revived in 1773. It was one of the first to give sailors maritime names such as Captain Mizen and Jack Hatchway. The theatre boom of the early nineteenth century produced many forgotten works, such as *Black-Eyed Susan* of around 1829, and the actor T P Cooke made a profession of impersonating a seaman on stage. But in general the theatre was a difficult medium for sea stories.

The earliest English novelists, Daniel Defoe and Jonathan Swift, both featured shipwreck in their most famous novels. Swift said almost nothing about shipboard life and concentrated on various fantasy worlds, but Defoe had enough material in *Robinson Crusoe* (1719–20) to inspire several generations of young men to take up seafaring. Of the mid eighteenth-century novelists, Tobias Smollett was a former naval surgeon and his anti-hero *Roderick Random* (1748) follows the same trade for a time, although he soon comes on shore to continue his adventures. The first true naval novelist in English was Captain Frederick Marryat, who

had served with some distinction in the wars against Napoleon. His books give a vivid picture of shipboard life with much characterisation based on real people, although their adventures are often fantastic. He was the most popular writer of adventure stories in the second quarter of the nineteenth century, though largely forgotten today. Robert Louis Stevenson was connected with the sea through his family of lighthouse engineers, but was far too frail to pursue a seafaring career himself. Among many other works he created *Treasure Island* (1883), perhaps the most famous sea story of all time. His characters, particularly the loveable rogue, Long John Silver, are among the most memorable. The characters' background among pirates is in the past and is understated, but it created a vogue for pirate novels that lasted well into the next century.

Josef Korzeniowski was born in Russian-occupied Poland in 1857 to revolutionary parents. Deciding on a seafaring career, he gravitated toward the British merchant marine, which was by far the largest in the world, and was naturalised in 1884, adapting one of his middle names to become Joseph Conrad. Many of his ships are clearly recognisable in his fiction.

ABOVE
J M W Turner's view shows fishing boats off Hastings in 1818. As always, the boats in the foreground are carefully composed and the background of the town and cliffs is ethereal.

Conrad signed on as second mate of the *Narcissus* in Bombay in April 1884. The crew included several characters who are easily recognisable in his novel *The Nigger of the Narcissus* of 1897. Conrad gave up the sea in 1894. His novels depict realistically the life of the deep-sea mariner at the end of the nineteenth century, when ships' crews were cut to the bone to compete with steam.

C S Forester (1899–1966) conceived his Captain Horatio Hornblower character while on passage in the West Indies, but apart from that his seafaring experience was slight and he did his meticulous research from the contemporary magazine *Naval Chronicle*. He published a dozen novels on Hornblower's fictional career between 1937 and his death and became one of the most popular novelists of his generation.

RIGHT
Geoff Hunt RSMA's painting for the cover of Patrick O'Brian's *The Mauritius Command* shows seamen working in the rigging of a ship with a squadron in the background. (Reproduced by kind permission of the artist)

Churchill read the first books during a transatlantic voyage in 1941 and telegraphed back, 'Hornblower admirable'. This caused consternation among officials, who thought it was the code name of a secret operation they had not been told about.

Forester opened a rich seam dealing with the sea captain in the days before radio, making his own decisions, leading a disparate crew and relying upon his initiative. Other writers in this genre included Dudley Pope, Alexander Kent and Richard Woodman, but the best known was Patrick O'Brian. Actually, he was an Englishman christened Patrick Gurr but his novels attracted a great deal of critical acclaim as well as popular success in Britain and the USA.

Music and the Sea

Commanders of large warships often relied on music to make their instructions clear. Medieval seals show trumpeters, and this was continued into the eighteenth century, when tiny trumpeters' cabins were provided on the poop decks of flagships. The drum was another way of issuing orders, and the expression 'beat to quarters', the order to go to action stations, reveals its origin. The best-known specifically nautical instrument was the boatswain's whistle or call, which is said to have originated in the Crusades and remained in use throughout the twentieth century. Its tinny sound and limited range do not produce great music but it is used to pipe a captain aboard or to send orders such as 'lash up and stow' and 'hoist away'.

For entertainment, singing and music always played a significant part in a seaman's life. Eighteenth-century naval sailors liked melancholy songs such as 'Admiral Hosier's Ghost', which describes death in the West Indies. Ships' fiddlers are often found on crew lists and they were highly popular. The sea shanty, however, was a feature of merchant navy life. Its dirge-like tune is not universally loved. Ships' officers tried to assemble bands on board, and there are reports of them pressing men out of other ships to keep up the supply of instrumentalists. In 1904 the Royal Marines took over the duty of providing the Royal Navy's bands and a battleship, for example, had about two dozen musicians. They might entertain the crew, but their main role was to play for functions on board and in parades ashore. In action they helped to man the transmitting station, a kind of gunnery computer. In the Merchant Navy seamen were left to their own devices, but large passenger ships have often employed bands and singers for passenger entertainment.

The sea has been the inspiration for many songs, including sentimental ones about a sailor parting from his loved one, and famous patriotic tunes such as *Rule Britannia, Heart of Oak*. Charles Dibdin (1745–1814) had no great connection with the sea himself but composed many songs such as *Poor Jack* and *Tom Bowling*. The interaction between the sailor and the music hall continued in the nineteenth century.

The most famous nautical dance, the Sailor's Hornpipe, evolved in the Victorian theatre and was later taken up by sailors.

The seafaring profession itself has not produced any great music, perhaps because conditions at sea do not encourage such work. But most of the great British composers have done some works relating to the sea – Ralph Vaughan Williams' *Sea Symphony* and Benjamin Britten's opera *Billy Budd*, for example.

Applied Art

Sailors and shipowners have tended to decorate their vessels since the earliest times, for example the dragon heads on Viking ships. By the early seventeenth century the ship had evolved a huge beakhead projecting from the bows, which had little practical function except as toilet accommodation for the crew. It was heavily decorated on its rails and with a wood statue, the figurehead. Its shape evolved over the years, but in the late seventeenth and early eighteenth centuries only the largest ships had an individual one. Other warships had a crowned lion until the 1740s, after which the figure tended to represent the name of the ship. Figureheads continued into the age of the clipper ship with *Cutty Sark's* famous rendering of the young witch Nannie, but very few were fitted in steamships.

The Ship Model

BETWEEN 1660 and about 1750 the best-known style of British ship model was the 'Navy Board' model, also known as the 'Admiralty' or 'Dockyard' model. It probably began as a fairly simple aid to design, but soon evolved into a highly decorated artefact. By 1740 it still had the un-planked bottom showing timbers, not arranged as they would be in the real ship, but in a stylised and old-fashioned pattern. The hull above the wales, just above the waterline, is planked and often painted with an elaborate frieze. The figurehead and its supporting rails are shown in the bows, but the stern is the most elaborate of all. The rudder and almost vertical sternpost are shown with the horizontal transoms, which make up part of the underwater structure of the stern. Above that is the lower counter decorated with painted curtains, and the upper counter. A three-decked ship has three rows of stern windows with the wardroom for the officers, the admiral's cabin and the captain's cabin on a flagship. The two upper decks have open galleries with balustrades, with a taffrail above covered with intricate carvings. Quarter galleries project from the side of the ship on either side. Despite their exterior finery, they served as toilet accommodation for the officers.

This model bears the name *Barfleur*, but it does not entirely match any ship of that name and in any case it was not common to paint names on the stern in 1740, so it may have been added later. Its dimensions and layout identify it as a typical 80-gun three-decker of around 1740

ABOVE
The figurehead of the *Barfleur* model. By 1740 it was becoming more common for each ship to have its own figurehead rather than the standard lion, but three-deckers like this always had individual figureheads.

RIGHT INSET
The richly-decorated stern of the model.

Though the figurehead survived longer than any other type of external carving, ships tended to have the sides covered with decoration in the seventeenth century. The most extreme example was Charles I's *Sovereign of the Seas*. For most of the eighteenth century the Admiralty struggled to keep the expense of ship decoration under control, but until about 1800 most ships had large carved figures on each side of the stern, with elaborate rails and carvings between them.

Ship models were not made for religious purposes in Britain as they were in Ancient Egypt and in parts of Europe. The first English ones date from the middle of the seventeenth century, when the Admiralty ordered scale models of each new ship to be built. They were made in a very elaborate style with each individual frame reproduced, then partially planked. Early in the seventeenth century a much simpler style of solid block model was developed for planning purposes, while the Navy Board model reached its peak in the first half of the century. It was replaced by a different style in which the hull was carved from the solid then planked, often with decorations in bone.

During the Napoleonic Wars, French and American prisoners of war in Britain made models in bone and sold them. Like all sailor-made models they were very accurate in rigging detail, but rather vague about the shape of the hull. Later in the century the shipbuilders of the Clyde, Mersey and north-east England evolved a new style of model. The hull was of fairly simple 'bread-and-butter' construction, with standard fittings such as guns and winches bought from suppliers, and features such as doors and hatches painted on. The 'builders' models' were produced economically and taken round the great international exhibitions of the age to promote the products of the yards.

Ceramics were used in two ways to commemorate maritime events. A merchant ship was usually owned by a number of small investors, who would order a plate or a set of cutlery to record the ship's launch or commissioning. Porcelain figures and jugs were also made to record great naval battles, to represent heroes or to show figures such as the typical seaman.

Seafaring exploits have inspired many other artefacts of great beauty. Medals are a relatively recent innovation, awarded to captains and admirals in the Napoleonic Wars, or to the ordinary seamen only since 1848. The gallantry medal, the Victoria Cross, was first won by Mate Charles David Lucas of HMS *Hecla* for his exploits in the Crimean War. Successful captains of the Napoleonic Wars were also presented with very elaborate swords by city corporations or by Lloyds of London.

Film and Television

Film and television can be difficult media for representing the sea. Full-sized ships are expensive to build or to hire, and models are often not realistic enough to gain the respect of the viewer. This did not deter the makers of the pirate films of the 1920s and 1930s. Fans were impressed enough with the new medium and were prepared to overlook a few faults. The first true 'war film' in the modern sense was perhaps *In Which We Serve* of 1943, made by Noel Coward and based very directly on the exploits of Lord Louis Mountbatten in HMS *Kelly*. It was much more subtle than the usual propaganda pieces, introducing issues such as boredom, fear and death, although its attitudes to class look ridiculously old-fashioned. War films of the 1940s and 1950s were able to use real ships left over from the conflict, for example the corvette *Coreopsis* used in the filming of *The Cruel Sea*. Nautical films tended to decline after that, until the 1990s when computer technology allowed a new kind of realism in such films as *Titanic* and *Master and Commander*.

Chapter 16
Britain in the Global Age

Britain was exhausted but optimistic with the end of the war in 1945, and at first the outlook was positive for the shipping and shipbuilding industries. Lost tonnage had to be replaced, and with the German and Japanese industries out of action, so British shipyards flourished. Shipping enjoyed an Indian summer and took up where it had left off before the war. The navy's role was being questioned in the nuclear age, but it soon found new tasks in the Cold War against the USSR and its allies and in dealing with the mess created by the liquidation of the British Empire.

The Revolution in Merchant Shipping

By the late 1950s, the world was changing rapidly. Road was replacing rail as the main means of land transport and the first motorways were about to open. The economic boom created the affluent society, with ever-increasing demand for consumer goods. In politics Winston Churchill, who offered nothing but 'blood, toil, tears and sweat' was succeeded by Harold Macmillan, who never quite said, 'You've never had it so good'. Japanese industry had recovered and West Germany was undergoing an 'economic miracle', which would place her at the forefront of European industry, including shipbuilding. The British Empire was coming to an end and the majority of colonies were given independence in the late 1950s and 1960s. Britain's economic future seemed to lie with Europe, and she applied to join the European Common Market for the first time in 1962. The world lived under a *Pax Americana*, which enforced free trade within the greater part of the world, while a sustained boom, which lasted until 1973, created a huge and highly competitive global market for shipping.

The British were not short of ideas. The origins of the roll-on roll-off ferry lay in wartime landing craft, but the first purpose-built ro-ro was the *Bardic Ferry*, launched on the Clyde in 1957. This was one way in which shipping could integrate with the rising importance of road transport, and ever-larger ferries were built for cross-channel and island routes over the next few decades. Another way of linking with road transport was to develop containers, which could be transported as easily by sea, road and rail. The first attempt at this was the *Container Venturer*, built in 1958. Designed for the route between the north of England and Northern Ireland, she carried round-topped 17-foot wooden containers of a type common on British rail and roads at the time. But concurrently the American company SeaLand was developing containers up to 40 feet long, which could be stacked one on top of the other and provided the basis for future development. The international container age began in 1966 when SeaLand's *Fairland* made the first transatlantic voyage. The older ports, where thousands of dockers laboured rather inefficiently to load or unload a ship over many days, were doomed.

Britain had never really been a leader in the oil tanker business, and her shipping industry was not ready for the great oil boom of the 1950s. Until then tankers were rarely more than 20,000 tons until the Japanese built the *Sinclaire Petrole* of 56,000 tons in 1956, followed by the first 100,000-ton ship in 1959, then 200,000 tons in 1966, and ships of more than half a million tons in the 1970s. British builders lagged behind and their yards were on restricted sites. The oil crisis of 1973 ended the worldwide expansion of tankers.

The British did lead the way in the development of gas carriers. The first purpose-built one was the bizarrely named *Methane Princess* of 1958. But again the industry, which supplies countries such as Japan with much of their power, is centred elsewhere. In fast craft, the British led the way in the development of the hovercraft, but it does not cope well with bad weather. The foil of the hydrofoil rides through the waves rather than over them, while large catamarans give good stability with little underwater resistance. The SWATH (Small Waterplane Area Twin Hull) is a variation of the catamaran with flotation cylinders deep in the water to avoid the effects of the waves and prevent seasickness.

The State of the Merchant Fleet

The post-war shipping industry was affected by the temporary closures of the Suez Canal after the wars of 1956 and 1967. This caused owners to look towards larger ships, while Greek magnates such as Aristotle Onassis and Stavros Niarchos built new shipping lines by buying Liberty ships, which had been mass-produced in the USA and Britain during the war, then ordering their own. British shipping remained reasonably constant in tonnage for 40 years after the war, with between 16 and 22 million tons owned. Much more was registered in the country after the government offered subsidies and credit in the late 1960s, to a maximum of 33 million tons in 1975–6. But British tonnage was more or less static, while world tonnage was increasing. Britain owned 22 per cent of world tonnage in 1948 and less than 5 per cent by 1983. Most of world tonnage by this time was registered under 'flags of convenience', initially in Panama, Honduras and Liberia. Shipowners could avoid high taxes, strict safety regulations, high wages and union interference as was found in the developed countries. Other major shipping lines are based in Japan, Taiwan and China. Most of the great British shipping lines disappeared through merger or liquidation. However, a recent revival has seen British tonnage quadruple in size since the year 2000.

More than 80 companies belong to the Chamber of Shipping, including BP Shipping, Shell, Maersk, Zodiac, P&O Nedlloyd and CP Ships. Today, British merchant shipping has a turnover in excess of £6.5 billion.

Ferry services to Europe, Ireland and to the British islands remain important and the ro-ro ferry links in well with the road transport system. The Channel Tunnel opened in 1994 but it did not undermine the volume of cross-channel trade by sea. More serious is the effect of cheap airline tickets, which have caused the closure of some services from Portsmouth to the continent.

By the 1960s the shipping industry was far more international than it had been at any time in the past, with good and bad effects on Britain. The country is more dependent on shipping than ever, with vast quantities of food, manufactures and oil being imported every year. The British standard of living depends very much on cheap and efficient shipping, and the cost of transporting goods from the Pacific, for example, is almost negligible.

New Ports

New practices and bigger ships meant new ports, and the decline of old ones. The ports of London, Liverpool, Bristol and Glasgow were close to city centres where land and labour were increasingly expensive, although Liverpool found a new lease of life as a general port, and ports of the mouth of the River Avon near Bristol have flourished in the last 15 years. Moreover, the

BELOW
The new hovercraft *Swift* of 165 tons prepares to enter service in Hoverlloyd's Ramsgate to Calais service in 1969.

new age favoured road transport over rail, and road vehicles are never happy in congested cities. In London, the major docks were closed by the 1980s and developed as housing and office space, but down river ports such as Tilbury and the Isle of Grain are growing.

Today's ports are further from the centre, and some are on the fringes of the country. Dover, the leading ferry port, is in the south-east where it provides the fastest crossing to France. At the other extreme of the country, the huge oil terminal at Sullom Voe in Shetland handled 50 million tons of cargo a year at its peak in 1988, making it the second port in the country. Container ports tend to be nearer the centres where the goods will be distributed – Felixstowe on the east coast, and Southampton on the south are both within easy reach of the main centres of population.

Ports have also become more specialised over the years. Some concentrate on ferry traffic, some on containers and some on oil. They use far less labour than before. A major container port like Felixstowe might employ about 2000 people compared with 23,000 in London in 1967.

Cold War and De-Colonisation

After 1945 it was evident that the Royal Navy would no longer 'rule the waves' as the largest navy in the world with a US Navy many times larger and a growing Soviet fleet. It adjusted to life as a significant part of the North Atlantic Treaty Organisation alliance, providing ships to counter the huge Soviet submarine fleet. But, in fact, the Cold War never became hot, and most of the Royal Navy's action has come from other issues around the world. It had to endure withdrawals in the post-colonial era, sometimes turning them around to its advantage, such as when the sloop *Amethyst* escaped from Chinese Communist guns in 1949. It has had many thankless tasks, for example when it patrolled the seas around Palestine to prevent illegal Jewish immigration in the late 1940s, or in three Cod Wars when it tried to protect British fishing rights in Icelandic waters, until wider issues led to a political compromise. It supported the United Nations with aircraft carriers during the Korean War of 1950–53, but was a very junior partner to the Americans. The nearest thing to an independent action in those years was the Suez affair, in which Britain and France landed troops in Egypt after President Nasser nationalised the Canal. But American opposition forced a quick withdrawal and the resignation of a prime minister. The navy carried out all these tasks with the greatest professionalism and skill, and maintained its morale in long and sometimes fruitless patrols.

The Falklands War of 1982 brought the navy back into prominence again. The Argentines invaded the islands and South Georgia on 2 April and Britain immediately sent out a Task Force led by the aircraft carriers *Hermes* and *Invincible*. An exclusion zone was declared round the islands but the Argentine cruiser *General Belgrano* was outside it when she was sunk by the submarine *Conqueror* as a continuing threat to the Task Force. The Argentine fleet stayed in port after that incident, but the Task Force was subjected to many air attacks, which sunk the destroyers *Sheffield* and *Coventry*. British forces landed in San Carlos Bay as two frigates were lost, followed by a container ship and a landing ship.

ABOVE
The Danish container ship *Maren Maersk* is loaded at Felixstowe. The overhead cranes are specially designed for container work and lift up to allow the ship to move in and out.

LEFT
A docker prepares to lift a sack of bark extract using hooks in 1945. Within 30 years such work would be obsolete.

very high efficiency, and its aircraft and missiles have a reach far beyond anything in the days of guns and torpedoes.

Modern Warships

In warships as in merchant ships, the British were full of ideas but often lacked the means to carry them out. The war had shown the dominance of the aircraft carrier, but the increasing speed and weight of the new jet aircraft made it very expensive to build and run. The Royal Navy developed the steam catapult to launch it and the mirror landing aid to replace the old batsman who signalled to guide the pilot on to the deck. It also hit on the idea of angling the deck a few degrees to port, allowing several kinds of operations to take place at once. But this required some conversion work of existing carriers, and the Americans developed it more quickly than the British. The country relied on war-built carriers for several decades, and the navy suffered a huge blow when a projected new carrier, codenamed CVA-01, was cancelled. But carriers came in through the back door. Three ships of the *Invincible* class, planned as helicopter carriers, were adapted to use the vertical take off Sea Harrier and this proved highly successful in the Falklands War. Two new and larger carriers are planned.

After the Second World War the navy experimented unsuccessfully with hydrogen test peroxide propulsion for submarines. This gave a good underwater performance but was too dangerous, and was overtaken by the American development of nuclear power. An exchange with the Americans led to the deployment of HMS *Dreadnought* in 1960 with an American reactor. Subsequently in 1962 the Prime Minister and US President agreed, at a meeting in Nassau, for the USA to supply Polaris missiles to Britain for inclusion in a NATO mulitlateral nuclear force. This necessitated the building of a fleet of four large submarines and the redevelopment of Faslane in Scotland to accommodate them. Since 1969 the Royal Navy has operated Britain's main nuclear deterrent, with at least one submarine continuously

The war had a triumphant ending as the islands were re-occupied. The British sailor was restored, for a time at least, as the hero of the people. The war, which lasted 72 days, cost 236 British and 655 Argentinian lives, but has not ended Argentina's claim to the islands.

The collapse of the USSR in 1991 changed the role of the navy yet again. Aircraft carriers are back in favour, partly due to their flexibility in land, sea and air operations. Amphibious operations are in fashion as it seems likely that work in support of the army will be important in the future. The modern navy is about a quarter of the size of the post war peak of 130,000 in 1952. It is less than half the size of that in 1982, at the time of the Falklands War. However, the Royal Navy remains proud of its

LEFT
The frigate HMS *Brave*, launched in Glasgow in 1983. She was one of the *Broadsword* class. These ships were regarded as innovative in carrying no main gun armament and relying on missiles. They were successful in the Falklands War, but guns would have proved useful and were restored in later classes.

at sea. Although it created a new role for the navy, some regarded it as a distraction from the real work in controlling the sea. Others outside the navy questioned the morality or the economics, especially after Polaris was replaced by the more expensive Trident in the 1990s and the end of the Soviet Union seemed to remove the rationale for it.

The older types of warship declined. The ship of the line and the battleship had dominated British naval thinking for three centuries. In 1960 the last one, HMS *Vanguard*, went to the breaker's yard. Cruisers lasted a little longer, but the destroyer had to reinvent itself as an anti-aircraft guided missile ship. The frigate became the most common surface warship, designed largely but not entirely for the anti-submarine role. The minesweeper has played a large role in the modern navy, and indeed mines have presented a very real threat, for example during the Iran-Iraq war in the 1980s. The largest class of ships since the war were the Ton class inshore minesweepers, and more than a hundred of them were built, to be replaced by more up-to-date models in later years.

The Decline of British Shipbuilding

British shipbuilders misjudged the post-war situation. Fearing that the economic boom would soon collapse, they failed to invest in new technology and were slow to adopt new techniques such as prefabrication and welding. The shipyards, founded in the previous century, were situated mostly on restricted sites in shallow rivers and surrounded by housing. Labour relations deteriorated and thousands of days were lost through strikes every year. Many investors believed, mistakenly, that world shipbuilding was likely to decline and many opportunities were lost, for example in cruise ships and oil rig support vessels. Shipbuilding also became a political football.

In 1968 a Labour government formed Upper Clyde Shipbuilders in an attempt to save what was left of shipbuilding in the area. In 1971 a Conservative government withdrew its subsidy, causing a famous 'work-in' which led to some concessions. In 1977 Labour nationalised the industry despite opposition from the owners. In 1984–5 British Shipbuilders lost £238 million and the Thatcher government privatised it. A few yards remained, building small ferries, gas

ABOVE

HMS *Bulwark* is the second of
a new class of assault ships,
launched in 2001 and to be
commissioned into the Royal
Navy in April 2005. She carries
up to six tanks and eight landing
craft, up to 700 troops and can
operate helicopters in support
of a landing.

carriers and warships, but the British had lost
many skills. Despite their traditional British
links, P&O and Cunard have to turn to
Germany, Italy, France and Japan to build high-
class passenger ships.

The Royal Dockyards began to contract with
the reduction of the Royal Navy. They were privatised in the 1980s. Chatham was closed in
1984 and became a Historic Dockyard. Threats
to close Portsmouth were averted and part of
the yard was let out to Vosper Thornycroft for
destroyer building. Part of the site, including the
world's greatest complex of historic ships and
maritime museums, became a heritage area.
Devonport Dockyard at Plymouth remained
intact but Rosyth in Scotland ceased to be a
naval base. The Faslane base on the other side
of Scotland, however, was vastly expanded to
cater for the new Trident submarines.

Maritime London

London remains the financial and administra-
tive centre of the maritime world. It benefits
from the decision of 1884, to standardise time
on Greenwich, which means that a trader in
London can do business with Tokyo in the
morning and New York in the afternoon of the
same day. Lloyd's of London is still the world
centre of insurance and Lloyd's Register is the
most important certification body, with a profound effect on the standards by which ships
are built and operated. *Lloyd's List* is the
world's premier daily shipping newspaper, supplemented by the weekly *Fairplay*. The
International Maritime Organisation, a United
Nations agency that regulates shipping, is based
on the south bank of the Thames. The Baltic
Exchange survived terrorist bombing in 1992
and is still the main world centre for ship charter. Most international contracts and charters
are agreed under British law, making London
courts the arbiters of any disputes. And, as a
legacy of the past, English is accepted as the
universal maritime language.

Maritime Heritage

With its rich seafaring history, it is no surprise
that Britain claims to be the world's leading
country for maritime heritage. Its many preserved ships include Nelson's *Victory* and the
clipper *Cutty Sark*. The National Historic Ships
Committee was formed in 1992 at the National
Maritime Museum to help secure the future of
a representative sample of Britain's most
important historic vessels. The Committee has
since created the National Register of Historic
Vessels, which lists 1200 historic craft from
small fishing boats to the SS *Great Britain* and
HMS *Belfast*. Other historic ships can be built
from original plans and research. Perhaps the
most popular and striking reconstruction is of
Cook's *Endeavour*. The most stunning event in
British nautical archaeology was the raising of
the *Mary Rose* in 1982. There are many other
wrecks in British waters, which are being thor-
oughly investigated and are already telling us
much about our maritime past. In maritime
history, Britain has an unrivalled record. The
Society for Nautical Research, set up in 1911,
was a pioneer in the field and the National
Maritime Museum is in many ways the largest
in the world, with the richest collections. Over
the last 30 years or so British historians have
produced a large and high-quality volume of
work, which has challenged many long-held

present day. It allowed Britain to develop into the greatest empire of its age, a fact which still causes discomfort, even shame, to many, and needs to be worked through the national psyche. Like all maritime nations, it allowed Britain to become cosmopolitan and broadminded. George Melly wrote of his petty officers in the wartime navy:

> Long association with the sea and its ports had given them a certain tolerant sophistication, part cynical but certainly affectionately so. They had learnt to mistrust the moral imperatives of any one place because they had seen them replaced by others, often equally rigid and ridiculous, elsewhere.

This was true of most seafarers, and tended to rub off on the peoples of port towns. At sea, sailors are deeply concerned with the safety of other sailors, even enemy ones. Ludovic Kennedy watched the sinking of the *Bismarck* and agreed with an officer who observed: '…surely all men are much the same when hurt'. This compassion, he thought, was 'shared by many British sailors that day, yet one rarely expressed by airmen who incinerate cities or by soldiers of those they kill in tanks'. The sea, a common highway, battleground and sometimes enemy for the whole of the world's seafaring population, produces its own comradeship even in the worst of circumstances.

The Royal Navy's relevance remains, although its focus has shifted from the Cold War to smaller, rapidly deployable forces, engaged in smaller conflicts, in littoral waters, around the world. The 'war on terror', whilst it has yet to produce any major British incident at sea, requires presence, engagement, and the ability to project military force globally. Merchant shipping is likely to grow, but at the moment there are no great technological changes on the horizon. There is likely to be increased concern about the maritime environment. Leisure use is likely to grow, at the risk of overcrowding in popular areas. But the British will remain a maritime people, not just because of the facts of geography or economics, but because of deeply ingrained attitudes.

assumptions, although it has to be admitted that mainstream historians still tend to neglect the maritime dimension, and the subject is only given its full due in a few universities. But our maritime heritage is all around us. It is etched into the landscape, it is in the siting and layout of towns, in the buildings, statues and monuments, and reveals itself in art and literature, and in the very language that we speak.

The Sea in the Future

What has Britain gained from nearly 10,000 years of island status? Mostly it has profited from a very close relationship with the sea, which has provided a route for invaders, immigrants, explorers, emigrants, conquerors and tourists. It has allowed the import of ideas and raw materials and the export of coal, manufactures and shipping services. For nearly 1000 years it has allowed the country to keep out enemies, and to take as much or as little part in Atlantic and European affairs as it wants to – a debate that dominates British politics to the

LEFT
The *Lutine* Bell at Lloyd's of London. Recovered from the wreck of a ship lost in 1793, it was traditionally rung once for bad news, for example that a ship had been lost, and twice for good news. Today it is mostly used on ceremonial occasions.

Gazetteer of Attractions

SCOTLAND

Aberdeen Maritime Museum
Shiprow, Aberdeen AB11 2BY
Tel: (01224) 337700
www.aagm.co.uk
Maritime museum with large exhibition area, including hands-on and interactive displays. The North Sea oil and gas industry is featured. Historic ship models.

Arbroath Signal Tower Museum
Arbroath, Angus DD11 1PU
Tel: (01241) 875598
Housed in Robert Stevenson's 1813 shore station of the Bell Rock Lighthouse, displays include a reconstructed fishing village street scene where models speak in the rich local dialect.

The Buckie Drifter Maritime Heritage Centre
Freuchny Road, Buckie, Banffshire AB56 1TT
Tel: (01542) 834646
www.moray.org/area/bdrifter/mbdrifter.html
Journey back in time to the days when herrings were 'king' and thousands of north-east fisher folk followed the shoals.

Clydebuilt (Scottish Maritime Museum Braehead)
Braehead Shopping Centre, Kings Inch Road, Glasgow G51 4BN
Tel: (0141) 886 1013
www.scottishmaritimemuseum.org
This dynamic new attraction on the River Clyde brings to life the story of Glasgow's development, from the tobacco lords in the 1700s right up to the 21st century.

Deep-Sea World
Battery Quarry, North Queensferry, Inverkeithing, Fife KY11 1JR
Tel: (01383) 411880
www.deepseaworld.com
Discover Scotland's triple award-winning aquarium. Enjoy a spectacular diver's-eye view of our marine environment in the world's longest underwater acrylic tunnel.

Denny Ship Model Experiment Tank (Scottish Maritime Museum Dumbarton)
Castle Street, Dumbarton, Ayrshire G02 1QS
Tel: (01389) 763444
www.scottishmaritimemuseum.org
Last surviving part of William Denny and Brothers shipyard restored to working condition, and still used for testing ships.

Discovery Point and RRS Discovery
Discovery Quay, Dundee DD1 4XA
Tel: (01382) 201245
www.rrsdiscovery.com
Discovery Point Centre contains audio-visual displays about Captain Scott's ship *Discovery* and includes a spectacular film show. Exhibits also depict Antarctic exploration.

Frigate *Unicorn* and RRS *Discovery*, Dundee.

Frigate Unicorn
Victoria Dock, Dundee DD1 3JA
Tel: (01382) 200900
www.frigateunicorn.org
Unicorn is Scotland's oldest historic ship. Launched in peacetime at Chatham, Kent, in 1824, the *Unicorn* was laid up in ordinary and roofed over at once. She is fully restored.

Inveraray Maritime Museum
Inveraray Pier, Inveraray, Argyll PA32 8UY
Tel: (01499) 302213
West Scotland maritime history with artefacts and archive film aboard an historic three-masted schooner. Also children's hands-on activities.

The Royal Yacht Britannia
Ocean Terminal, Leith Docks, Edinburgh EH6 6JJ
Tel: (0131) 555 5566
www.royalyachtbritannia.co.uk
Britannia, moored in Edinburgh, is open all year as a visitor attraction and hospitality venue.

Scottish Fisheries Museum
St Ayles, Harbourhead, Anstruther, Fife KY10 3AB
Tel: (01333) 310628
www.scotfishmuseum.org
The many facets of fisher-folk life are portrayed in the museum, including the tragedies they face. The museum currently has 15 full-size boats in the collection. Includes the fifie *Reaper*.

Scottish Maritime Museum, Irvine
Harbourside, Irvine, Ayrshire KA12 8QE
Tel: (01294) 278283
Built in 1872, the Linthouse Engine Shop holds a substantial part of the Museum's collections in open store. Shipyard worker's flat and historic vessels can also be visited.

The Tall Ship at Glasgow Harbour
100 Stobcross Road, Glasgow G3 8QQ
Tel: (0141) 222 2513
www.thetallship.com
Restored to her former glory, the *Glenlee* is one of only five remaining Clydebuilt sailing ships still afloat in the world. Discover what life was like aboard a tall ship.

ENGLAND'S NORTH COUNTRY

The Albert Dock
22 Edward Pavilion, Albert Dock, Liverpool L3 4AF
Tel: (0151) 708 7334
www.albertdock.com
Britain's largest Grade I Listed historic building. Restored four-sided dock including shops, bars, restaurants, a marina and maritime museum.

Arctic Corsair
Rear of Streetlife Museum, High Street, Hull, East Riding of Yorkshire HU1 1PS
Tel: (01482) 613902
www.hullcc.gov.uk/museums
Relive the backbreaking and dangerous work that took place thousands of miles from home just to put fresh fish on the nation's tables.

Bamburgh Castle
Bamburgh, Northumberland NE69 7DF
Tel: (01668) 214545
www.bamburghcastle.com
Magnificent coastal castle, completely restored in 1900. Collections of china, porcelain, furniture, paintings, arms and armour.

Bridlington Harbour Heritage Museum
Harbour Road, Bridlington, East Riding of Yorkshire YO15 2NR
Tel: (01262) 608346
www.bscps.com
Photographs, harbour history models, diorama of the fishing techniques, video presentation.

Captain Cook Birthplace Museum
Stewart Park, Marton, Middlesbrough, Cleveland TS7 8AT
Tel: (01642) 311211
www.captcook-ne.co.uk
Discover why Captain Cook is the world's most famous navigator and explorer. Find out about life below decks in the 18th century. Temporary exhibitions.

Captain Cook Memorial Museum
Grape Lane, Whitby, North Yorkshire YO22 4BA
Tel: (01947) 601900
www.cookmuseumwhitby.co.uk
A 17th-century house where James Cook lodged as an apprentice seaman with a rich collection of original exhibits about his life and voyages.

The Albert Dock and Liver Building, Liverpool.

Captain Cook Schoolroom Museum
101 High Street, Great Ayton, Middlesbrough, Cleveland TS9 6NB
Tel: (01642) 722966
www.captaincookschoolroommuseum.co.uk
The museum is housed in two rooms of the Postgate School, built in 1704, where James Cook received his early education.

The Dock Museum
North Road, Barrow-in-Furness, Cumbria LA14 2PW
Tel: (01229) 894444
www.dockmuseum.org.uk
Spectacular modern museum built over an original Victorian dry dock. Galleries include multimedia interactives, and impressive ship models.

Filey Museum
8-10 Queen Street, Filey, North Yorkshire YO14 9HB
Tel: (01723) 515013
Fishing, lifeboat, rural, domestic, local and photographic items. Victorian drawing room. Seashore displays of shells, fossils and stones. Garden with salmon coble/baiting shed.

Fleetwood Museum
Queens Terrace, Fleetwood, Lancashire FY7 6BT
Tel: (01253) 876621
www.nettingthebay.org.uk
Fleetwood Museum has excellent displays on the maritime heritage of Fleetwood and the Lancashire coast.

Hartlepool Historic Quay
Maritime Avenue, Hartlepool, Cleveland TS24 0XZ
Tel: (01429) 860006 (24hr information)
www.destinationhartlepool.com
Hartlepool Historic Quay is an exciting reconstruction of a seaport of the 1800s with buildings and a lively quayside, authentically reconstructed.

HM Bark Endeavour
Castlegate Quay Heritage Project, Watersports Centre, Moat Street, Stockton-on-Tees, Cleveland TS18 3AZ
Tel: (01642) 608038
www.castlegatequay.co.uk
Heritage visitor attraction on full-size replica of Captain James Cook's ship *Endeavour*. Situated on the river with children's games area.

HMS Trincomalee
Jackson Dock, Hartlepool, Cleveland TS24 0SQ
Tel: (01429) 223193
www.hms-trincomalee.co.uk
HMS *Trincomalee*, built in 1817, is the oldest ship afloat in Britain, which provides a unique experience of navy life two centuries ago.

Historic Warships at Birkenhead
East Float, Dock Road, Birkenhead, Merseyside CH41 1DJ
Tel: (0151) 650 1573
www.historicwarships.org
Home to the former Royal Navy submarine HMS *Onyx*, frigate HMS *Plymouth*, minehunter HMS *Bronington* and the U-boat *U534* raised from the sea bed 48 years after sinking by a depth charge.

Lancaster Maritime Museum
Custom House, St George's Quay, Lancaster LA1 1RB
Tel: (01524) 64637
www.lancaster.gov.uk/council/museums
A custom house in a delightful riverside setting, designed by Richard Gillow and built in 1764. Displays of 18th-century trade with West Indies and the fishing communities of Morecambe.

Maritime Museum Hull
Queen Victoria Square, Hull, East Riding of Yorkshire HU1 3DX
Tel: (01482) 613902
www.hullcc.gov.uk/museums
Whaling, fishing and trawling exhibits. Local history on the evolution of trawling and Hull's docklands. Various temporary exhibitions.

Maryport Maritime Museum
1 Senhouse Street, Maryport, Cumbria CA15 6AB
Tel: (01900) 813738
www.allerdale.gov.uk
Local history collection emphasising Maryport's maritime tradition, including Fletcher Christian and the *Titanic*. Also items of general maritime interest.

Merseyside Maritime Museum
Albert Dock, Liverpool L3 4AQ
Tel: (0151) 478 4499
www.merseysidemaritimemuseum.org.uk
Liverpool's seafaring heritage brought to life in the historic Albert Dock.

National Fishing Heritage Centre
Alexandra Dock, Grimsby, North East Lincolnshire DN31 1UZ
Tel: (01472) 323345
www.nelincs.gov.uk
Experience the reality of life on a deep-sea trawler. Interactive games and displays, and children's area.

RNLI Grace Darling Museum
Radcliffe Road, Bamburgh, Northumberland NE69 7AE
Tel: (01668) 214465
Museum commemorates the rescue, by Grace and her father, of the nine survivors from the wreck of the *Forfarshire*. Many original relics, the coble used in the rescue, paintings and books.

RNLI Zetland Lifeboat Museum
5 King Street, Redcar, North Yorkshire TS10 3PF
Tel: (01642) 494311
www.redcarlifeboat.org.uk
Listed building housing the *Zetland*, the oldest surviving lifeboat in the world, built in 1802 by Henry Greathead. Fishing history, models, photographs, paintings and cards.

The Rum Story
27 Lowther Street, Whitehaven, Cumbria CA28 7DN
Tel: (01946) 592933
www.rumstory.co.uk
The Rum Story is the world's first exhibition depicting the unique story of the British rum trade in the original Jefferson family's wine merchant premises.

Saltburn Smugglers Heritage Centre
Old Saltburn, Near the Ship Inn, Saltburn-by-the-Sea, Cleveland TS12 1HF
Tel: (01287) 625252
The Saltburn Smugglers is set in authentic fishermen's cottages. Step back into Saltburn's past and experience the authentic sights, sounds and smells.

Sea Life and Marine Sanctuary
Scalby Mills, Scarborough, North Yorkshire YO12 6RP
Tel: (01723) 373414
www.sealifeeurope.com
At the Sea Life Centre you have the opportunity to meet creatures that live in and around the seas of the British Isles, ranging from starfish and crabs to rays and seals.

Souter Lighthouse
Coast Road, Whitburn, South Shields, Sunderland SR6 7NH
Tel: (0191) 529 3161
www.nationaltrust.org.uk
The world's most advanced lighthouse when built in 1871. Climb the tower and visit the engine room and Victorian keeper's cottage. Hands-on activities and events.

Trinity House, Newcastle upon Tyne

Broad Chare, Newcastle upon Tyne NE1 3DQ
Tel: (0191) 232 8226
www.trinityhousenewcastle.org.uk
Maritime organisation housed in a Listed buildings complex dating from the 14th century, with a collection of maritime artefacts.

Western Approaches

1 Rumford Street, Liverpool L2 8SZ
Tel: (0151) 227 2008
Visit the former top-secret underground headquarters for the Battle of the Atlantic in the heart of Liverpool. A complete restoration with original artefacts.

Whitby Lifeboat Museum (RNLI)

Pier Road, Whitby, North Yorkshire YO21 3PU
Tel: (01947) 602001
Last pulling lifeboat of the RNLI, now preserved; models of lifeboats and other types of vessel; diorama of the *Rohilla* wreck, the hospital ship that sank on her way to pick up soldiers from Dunkirk in 1914; local history of the Whitby RNLI.

Whitby Museum

Pannett Park, Whitby, North Yorkshire YO21 1RE
Tel: (01947) 602908
www.durain.demon.co.uk
Captain Cook material, whaling, ship models, Whitby jet ornaments, local history, William Scoresby, geology and fossils, archaeology, bygones and costumes.

Withernsea Lighthouse Museum

Hull Road, Withernsea, East Riding of Yorkshire HU19 2DY
Tel: (01964) 614834
Magnificent view of Withernsea from the top of the 127-foot-high lighthouse. Local history museum and the Kay Kendall Memorial Museum. HM Coastguard and RNLI collection.

ENGLAND'S HEARTLAND

Alfred Corry Museum

Ferry Road, 10 The Oaklands, Southwold, Suffolk IP18 6RD
Tel: (01502) 722103
www.http://freespace.virgin.net/david.cragie
The old Cromer lifeboat station transported by sea to Southwold. The 110-year-old station has been restored and now houses the old Southwold lifeboat, *Alfred Corry*.

Brightlingsea Museum

1 Duke Street, Brightlingsea, Colchester, Essex CO7 0EA
Tel: (01206) 303185
www.brightlingsea-town.co.uk/history/museum.htm
The maritime and social history museum of Brightlingsea (a limb of the Cinque Port of Sandwich) with collections relating to the town's Cinque Port connections.

Cromer Museum

East Cottages, Tucker Street, Cromer, Norfolk NR27 9HB
Tel: (01263) 513543
www.museums.norfolk.gov.uk
A late-Victorian fisherman's cottage with displays of local history (fishing, bathing resort), geology, natural history and archaeology.

Southwold on the Suffolk coast.

Dunwich Underwater Exploration Exhibition

The Orford Craft Shop, Orford, Woodbridge, Suffolk IP12 2LN
Tel: (01394) 450678
Exhibits show progress in the underwater exploration of the former city and underwater studies off the Suffolk coast. Attraction is not suitable for small children.

The Excelsior Trust

Harbour Road, Oulton Broad, Lowestoft, Suffolk NR32 3LY
Tel: (01502) 585302
www.excelsiortrust.co.uk
Traditional sailing trawler which offers daysails out of Lowestoft, Ipswich and Weymouth for individuals and groups.

Felixstowe Museum

Landguard Point, Viewpoint Road, Felixstowe, Suffolk IP11 7JG
Tel: (01394) 674355
www.landguard.com/museum1.htm

The museum is housed in the Ravelin block adjacent to Landguard Fort. There are exhibits covering local, social and military history of the area.

Harwich Lifeboat Museum

Timberfields, Off Wellington Road, Harwich, Essex CO12 3EJ
Tel: (01255) 503429
www.harwich-society.com
The Harwich Lifeboat Museum contains the last Clacton offshore 37-foot lifeboat, the Oakley class and a fully-illustrated history of lifeboat service in Harwich.

Harwich Maritime Museum

Low Lighthouse, Harbour Crescent, Harwich, Essex CO12 3NJ
Tel: (01255) 503429
www.harwich-society.com
A museum with special displays related to the Royal Navy and commercial shipping with fine views over the continuous shipping movements in the harbour.

Harwich Redoubt Fort

Behind 29 Main Road, Harwich, Essex CO12 3LT
Tel: (01255) 503429
www.harwich-society.com
An anti-Napoleonic circular fort commanding the harbour. Eleven guns on battlements.

Henry Blogg Museum

The Old Boathouse, The Promenade, Cromer, Norfolk NR27 9HE
Tel: (01263) 511294
Second World War Watson class lifeboat *H F Bailey*, Bloggs boat, which saved 500 lives between 1935 and 1945.

The Lifeboat Station

Boathouse, Tower Esplanade, Skegness, Lincolnshire PE25 3HH
Tel: (01754) 763011
Visitors may see the offshore and inshore lifeboats with group visits by appointment or a conducted tour if convenient.

Lowestoft and East Suffolk Maritime Museum

Sparrows Nest Park, Whapload Road, Lowestoft, Suffolk NR32 1XG
Tel: (01502) 561963
The museum houses models of fishing and commercial ships, shipwright's tools, fishing gear, a

The Pier and Promenade at Cromer.

lifeboat display, an art gallery and a drifter's cabin with models of fishermen.

Maritime Exhibition

King's Lynn Tourist Information Centre, Custom House, Purfleet Quay, King's Lynn, Norfolk
PE30 1HP
Tel: (01553) 763044
Visit King's Lynn's most famous landmark, the Custom House, and discover the town's colourful maritime history.

Mincarlo Trawler

Yacht Basin, Lowestoft Harbour, Lowestoft, Suffolk
Tel: (01502) 565234
www.lydiaeva.org.uk
Mincarlo was launched in 1962; *Lydia Eva* steam drifter is currently out of service. Both vessels are preserved by a trust as museums of the local fishing industries.

Mundesley Maritime Museum

Beach Road, Mundesley, Norwich NR11 8BG
Tel: (01263) 720879
The former Coastguard contains photographs, prints and artefacts illustrating Mundesley's maritime and village history. The first floor has been reinstated as a lookout.

National Sea Life Centre

The Water's Edge, Brindley Place, Birmingham
B1 2HL
Tel: (0121) 643 6777
www.sealifeeurope.com
Marvel at over 3000 sea creatures displayed in a magical underwater setting, complete with the world's first 360-degree transparent, tubular, underwater walk-through tunnel.

Norfolk Nelson Museum

21 South Quay, Great Yarmouth, Norfolk NR30 2RG
Tel: (01493) 850698
www.nelson-museum.co.uk
Visit the Norfolk Nelson Museum to find out about Admiral Lord Horatio Nelson and his life and career on land and at sea.

Royal Naval Patrol Service Association Museum

Sparrows Nest, Lowestoft, Suffolk NR32 1XG
Tel: (01502) 586250
A museum with photographs of models of Second World War officers and crews, minesweepers and anti-submarine vessels. Also models of American and British mine sweepers.

The Seal Sanctuary

North End, Mablethorpe, Lincolnshire LN12 1QG
Tel: (01507) 473346
A wildlife sanctuary in gardens and natural dunes with the emphasis on Lincolnshire wildlife, past and present, and the Seal Trust Wildlife Hospital.

Sheringham Museum

Station Road, Sheringham, Norfolk NR26 8RE
Tel: (01263) 821871
Local social history museum. Displays on lifeboats and fishing heritage, boat-building, the 1.5-million-year-old 'Weybourne Elephant', flint picking.

Sutton Hoo

Tranmer House, Sutton Hoo, Woodbridge, Suffolk
IP12 3DJ
Tel: (1394) 389714
www.nationaltrust.org.uk
Exhibition hall houses a full-size reconstruction of the burial chamber of the Anglo-Saxon ship. New in 2005 is an exhibition of some of the original artefacts from the excavation, on loan by kind permission of the British Museum.

Thames Barge Heritage Centre

SB *Glenway*, Cooks Barge Yard, The Hythe, Maldon, Essex CM9 5HN
Tel: (01621) 857567
www.cooksbargeyard.co.uk
Cooks Barge Yard Heritage Centre tells the story of the Thames barge from evolution in the early 1800s to its heyday at the turn of the twentieth century.

Thames Sailing Barge Trust

Crosstrees, The Downs, Maldon, Essex CM9 5HR
www.bargetrust.org
Preservation of barges *Centaur* and *Pudge* in sailing condition to promote and teach sailing, handling and maintenance of the craft.

SOUTH AND SOUTH-EAST ENGLAND

Allchorn Pleasure Boats

Eastbourne Beach (between the pier and bandstand) and Marina, Eastbourne, East Sussex BN21
Tel: (01323) 410606
www.allchornpleasureboats.co.uk
Pleasure cruises lasting 45 minutes in historic/locally-built classic Sussex-style boats from Eastbourne beach to Holywell, Beachy Head and Cow Gap. Also lifeboat cruises on the former RNLB *The Robert*.

Bembridge Lifeboat Station

Lane End, Bembridge, Isle of Wight PO35 5ST
Tel: (01983) 875127
Off-shore lifeboat on slipway at end of 250-yard pier. This is a fully operational lifeboat. All viewings are strictly subject to operational requirements.

Bembridge Maritime Museum Isle of Wight Shipwreck Centre

Providence House, Sherborne Street, Bembridge, Isle of Wight PO35 5SB
Tel: (01983) 872223
www.iowight.com/shipwrecks
A museum devoted to displaying nautical heritage. Displays of shipwrecks, salvage, pirate treasure, early and modern diving equipment.

Chart Gunpowder Mills

Westbrook Walk, Faversham, Kent ME13 7SE
Tel: (01795) 534542
www.faversham.org
Watermills that are the oldest gunpowder mills left in Britain. They were once part of the Royal Gunpowder Factory supplying Nelson and Wellington.

Chatley Heath Semaphore Tower

Pointers Road, Cobham, Surrey KT11 1PQ
Tel: (01372) 458822
A restored historic semaphore tower displaying the history of overland naval communications in early 19th century, set in woodland. Working semaphore mast and models.

Chicheley Hall

Newport Pagnell, Buckinghamshire MK16 9JJ
Tel: (01234) 391252
www.chicheleyhall.co.uk
Georgian house, unchanged since the 18th century. Contains many items of memorabilia of Admiral the Earl Beatty, head of the Battle Cruiser Group in the First World War.

The Classic Boat Museum

Newport Harbour, Seaclose Quay, Newport, Isle of Wight PO30 2EF
Tel: (01983) 533493
www.classicboatmuseum.org
A collection of beautiful boats of historic interest including the 1887 rowing lifeboat with engines, equipment and memorabilia. Working shed where boats are being restored.

Court Hall Museum

Court Hall, High Street, Winchelsea, East Sussex
TN36 4EU
Tel: (01797) 226382
A small local museum with exhibits on Winchelsea, the Cinque Ports and their history. Maps, seals, pictures, coins, weights and measures and local pottery are all on display.

Freshwater Bay, Isle of Wight.

Working boats on the beach at Hastings.

Cowes Maritime Museum

Bookford Road, Cowes, Isle of Wight PO31 7SG
Tel: (01983) 823847
www.iwight.com
Museum containing boats, paintings, and models
depicting the maritime history of Cowes and the
Isle of Wight.

Cutty Sark Clipper Ship

King William Walk, Greenwich, London SE10 9HT
Tel: (020) 8858 3445
www.cuttysark.org.uk
The world's sole surviving tea clipper ship.
Explore all decks and see the relics and famous
figureheads.

Deal Maritime and Local History Museum

22 St Georges Road, Deal, Kent CT14 6BA
Tel: (01304) 381344
Exhibits relating to the history of Deal, especially
maritime. Boat models, equipment, photographs
and charts. Periodic exhibitions.

Dolphin Sailing Barge Museum

Crown Quay Lane, Sittingbourne, Kent ME10 3SN
Tel: (01795) 424132
www.kentaccess.org.uk
Explore the age of the sailing barge. See surviving
barges undergoing repair or restoration in our basin.

Emsworth Museum

10B North Street (above the Fire Station),
Emsworth, Hampshire PO10 7DD
Tel: (01243) 378091 (weekends only)
www.emsworthmuseum.org.uk
Formerly the offices of Old Warblington District
Council dating from 1900. Displays reflect life in
Emsworth and include P G Wodehouse memorabil-
ia and artefacts on yachting legend, Sir Peter Blake.

Explosion! Museum of Naval Firepower

Priddy's Hard, Gosport, Hampshire PO12 4LE
Tel: (023) 9250 5600
www.explosion.org.uk
The amazing story of naval firepower, from gunpowder to the Exocet, in an exciting new visitor
experience for all the family on the shores of
Portsmouth Harbour.

Fishermen's Museum

Rock-a-Nore Road, Hastings, East Sussex
TN34 3DW
Tel: (01424) 461446
A former fishermen's church by the old net shops,
now a museum on local fishing with ship models,
nets, old photographs and the lugger *Enterprise*,
which was built in 1912.

Fort Victoria Sunken History Exhibition

Fort Victoria Country Park, Off Westhill Road,
Yarmouth, Isle of Wight PO41 0RR
Tel: (01983) 760283
www.fortvictoria.co.uk
Exhibition on local marine archaeology, especially
on the excavation of a local 16th-century wreck.
Learn how the Solent was flooded after the last
ice age.

Golden Hinde

St Mary Overie Dock, Cathedral Street, London
SE1 9DE
Tel: (020) 7403 0123
www.goldenhinde.co.uk
Full-scale reconstruction of Sir Francis Drake's
sailing galleon in which he completed England's
first circumnavigation of the globe.

HMS Belfast

Morgan's Lane, Tooley Street, London SE1 2JH
Tel: (020) 7940 6300
www.iwm.org.uk
Second World War cruiser, now a floating naval
museum on the Thames, with nine decks to
explore.

HMS Victory Flagship Portsmouth

Porters Lodge, College Road, HM Naval Base,
Portsmouth, Hampshire PO1 3LJ
Tel: (023) 9272 3111
www.historicdockyard.co.uk
HMS *Victory*, Vice-Admiral Lord Nelson's flagship at Trafalgar. Memorable tour of his cabin,
the cockpit where he died, and the sombre gun
decks where men lived.

HMS Warrior 1860 Portsmouth

Victory Gate, HM Naval Base, Portsmouth,
Hampshire PO1 3QX
Tel: (023) 9229 1379
www.historicdockyard.co.uk
The world's first iron-hulled, armoured battleship.
Four decks completely restored to show life in the
Victorian navy of 1860. Featuring cabins, ward-
room, engine and cannon.

The Historic Dockyard Chatham

Dock Road, Chatham, Kent ME4 4TZ
Tel: (01634) 823800
www.chdt.org.uk
Maritime heritage site with stunning architecture
and displays including Britain's last Second World
War destroyer *Cavalier* and the sloop *Gannet*,
plus RNLI exhibition.

Holyrood Church

High Street, Southampton, Hampshire
Tel: (023) 8063 5904
Medieval church that was bombed in the
Second World War. The ruins are now a memo-
rial to the men of the Merchant Navy who died
in that war. Also houses the Merchant Navy's
Titanic memorial.

Imperial War Museum

Lambeth Road, London SE1 6HZ
Tel: (020) 7416 5000
www.iwm.org.uk
The Imperial War Museum seeks to provide for
and to encourage the study and understanding
of the history of modern war and 'war time
experience'.

The Lifeboat Museum

King Edward Parade, Eastbourne, East Sussex
BN21 4BY
Tel: (01323) 730717
A comprehensive collection of lifeboats housed in
the former boathouse, plus ships in bottles, dis-
plays of lifesaving equipment and photographs.

London Aquarium

County Hall, Riverside Building, London SE1 7PB
Tel: (020) 7967 8000
www.londonaquarium.co.uk
Dive down deep beneath the Thames and sub-
merge yourself in one of Europe's largest displays
of aquatic life.

Margate Lifeboat House

The Harbour, Margate, Kent CT9 1HG
Tel: (01843) 221613
The Lifeboat House accommodates two lifeboats,
one offshore, one inshore and displays of exhibits
and service boards depicting the history of the
station from 1864.

Maritime Museum, Ramsgate

The Clock House, Pier Yard, Royal Harbour,
Ramsgate, Kent CT11 8LS
Tel: (01843) 587765
www.ekmt.tonet.co.uk
Four galleries devoted to local and national mar-
itime heritage, history of navigation, relics from
Goodwin Sands wrecks, RNLI, historic ship col-
lection, restored dry dock.

The *Golden Hinde*, London.

The Painted Hall, Old Royal Naval College, Greenwich.

Marlipins Museum

High Street, Shoreham-by-Sea, West Sussex
BN43 5DA
Tel: (01273) 462994
www.sussexpast.co.uk
Twelfth-century secular building with architectural features housing museum of the history of Shoreham as a port. Maritime paintings, models. Occasional special exhibitions.

Mary Rose Ship Hall and Museum Flagship Portsmouth

HM Naval Base, Portsmouth, Hampshire PO1 3LJ
Tel: (023) 9281 2931
www.historicdockyard.co.uk
The Ship Hall is devoted to the restoration and conservation of Henry VIII's warship. The Museum displays cannon, longbow, gold, tankards and game boards excavated from the wreck and includes a film and slide presentation on the sinking and raising of the *Mary Rose*.

Museum in Docklands

1 Warehouse, West India Quay, Hertsmere Road, London E14 4AL
Tel: 0870 444 3857
www.museumindocklands.org.uk
The Museum in Docklands explores the story of London's river, port and people from Roman times to recent regeneration.

Museum of Smuggling History

Botanic Garden, Ventnor, Isle of Wight PO38 1UL
Tel: (01983) 853677
www.smuggling-museum.co.uk
Seven hundred years of smuggling methods, including ingenious ways and the most unlikely things smuggled.

National Maritime Museum

Greenwich, London SE10 9NF
Tel: (020) 8858 4422
www.nmm.ac.uk
Explains Britain's worldwide maritime influence through its explorers, traders, migrants and naval power. Features on ship models, costume, and the ecology of the sea. Includes the Royal Observatory, Greenwich.

Newhaven Local and Maritime Museum

Paradise Park, Avis Road, Newhaven, East Sussex BN9 0DH
Tel: (01273) 612530
www.newhavenmuseum.co.uk
A local history museum with exhibits about Newhaven's maritime heritage. There is also a unique photographic and video collection of Newhaven's history.

North Foreland Lighthouse

Broadstairs, Kent CT10 3NW
www.trinityhouse.co.uk
A working historic lighthouse with the first light established in 1499. It was the last manned lighthouse in Britain. Converted to automatic operation in 1998.

The Old Lighthouse Dungeness

Dungeness, Romney Marsh, Kent TN29 9NA
Tel: (01797) 321300
www.dungenesslighthouse.btinternet.co.uk
Lighthouse with 167 steps to the top. Visitors can see how lantern was worked and cleaned when in use.

Old Royal Naval College

Cutty Sark Gardens, Greenwich, London SE10 9LW
Tel: (020) 8269 4791
www.greenwichfoundation.org.uk
Christopher Wren's 18th-century masterpiece and former naval pensioner's hospital is now open to explore its grounds, Painted Hall, Chapel and visitor centre.

Old Town Hall Museum

High Street, Hastings, East Sussex TN34 3EW
Tel: (01424) 781166
www.hmag.org.uk
Housed in a Regency town hall, the displays include seaside holidays, wartime, fishing, Victorian life, smuggling, Titus Oates, the Cinque Ports and the Hastings mint.

Portsmouth Cathedral

High Street, Portsmouth, Hampshire PO1 2HH
Tel: (023) 9282 3300
www.portsmouthcathedral.org.uk
Maritime cathedral with strong seafaring links. Tomb of unknown sailor from the *Mary Rose*. D-Day memorial window.

Portsmouth Historic Dockyard

Visitor Centre, College Road, HM Naval Base, Portsmouth, Hampshire PO1 3LJ
Tel: (023) 9286 1533
www.historicdockyard.co.uk
The Dockyard is home to Action Stations, *Mary Rose* exhibition, HMS *Victory*, HMS *Warrior*, the Royal Naval Museum, 'Warships by water' harbour tours, Dockyard Apprentice exhibition.

Royal Marines Museum

Southsea, Hampshire PO4 9PX
Tel: (023) 9281 9385
www.royalmarinesmuseum.co.uk
History of the Royal Marines from 1664 to present day. Jungle and trench warfare sight and sound exhibitions. D-Day, Falklands' cinemas and supporting exhibitions.

Royal Naval Museum Flagship Portsmouth

Porter's Lodge, HM Naval Base, Portsmouth, Hampshire PO1 3LJ
Tel: (023) 9286 1533
www.historicdockyard.co.uk
The only museum in Britain devoted to the overall history of the Royal Navy. Displays cover the past 1000 years of naval history.

RNLI Lifeboat Station

Denge Beach, Dungeness, Kent TN29 9ND
Tel: (01797) 320317
Visitors can see the Royal National Lifeboat Institution lifeboat *Pride and Spirit*, a Mersey class, 12-metre-long boat which offers a top speed of 17 knots.

Royal Navy Submarine Museum

Haslar Jetty Road, Gosport, Hampshire PO12 2AS
Tel: (023) 9252 9217
www.rnsubmus.co.uk
HM submarine *Alliance*, HM submarine No. 1 (Holland 1), midget submarines, models of every type of submarine from the earliest days to the present nuclear age.

St Margaret's Church

Parliament Square, London SW1P 3JX
Tel: (020) 7654 4840
www.westminster-abbey.org
A fine 16th-century building with notable medieval and modern stained glass. Burial place of Sir Walter Raleigh and parish church of the House of Commons.

St Margaret's Museum

Beach Road, St Margaret's Bay, Dover, Kent CT15 6DZ
Tel: (01304) 851737
www.baytrust.org.uk
A museum with items of local and marine interest, covering the First World War and Second World War periods. Figureheads and temporary exhibitions.

St Mary's Church, Rotherhithe

St Marychurch Street, London SE16 4JE
Tel: (020) 7231 2465
Early 18th-century church, with memorials and other items from the maritime history of the area.

Seaford Museum

Martello Tower, Esplanade, Seaford, East Sussex BN25 1JH
Tel: (01323) 898222
www.seafordmuseum.org
A converted Martello Tower with displays and exhibits on Seaford and the sea.

Shipwreck Heritage Centre

Rock-a-Nore Road, Hastings, East Sussex TN34 3DW
Tel: (01424) 437452
Maritime museum with 3000 years of historic treasures from local shipwrecks. Audiovisual show 'A Shipwreck Adventure', push button videos, live RADAR, weather satellite pictures.

A Smugglers Adventure at St Clement's Caves

West Hill, Hastings, East Sussex TN34 3HY
Tel: (01424) 422964
www.discoverhastings.co.uk
An extensive exhibition of 18th-century smuggling, housed in 2000 square metres of caves. Exhibition, museum, video theatre, extensive Adventure Walk incorporating dramatic special effects.

Southampton Maritime Museum

Wool House, Town Quay, Southampton, Hampshire
SO14 2AR
Tel: (023) 8022 3941
www.southampton.gov.uk/leisure/heritage
Medieval stone warehouse with timber roof.
Exhibitions on the port of Southampton, ship
models including ocean liners. A permanent exhi-
bition on the *Titanic* and Southampton.

Whitstable Museum and Gallery

Oxford Street, Whitstable, Kent CT5 1DB
Tel: (01227) 276998
www.whitstable-museum.co.uk
A coastal museum exploring the seafaring traditions of the town with special features on divers,
shipbuilders and oyster-fishers. Gallery with regu-
larly changing exhibitions.

ENGLAND'S WEST COUNTRY

Brixham Heritage Museum

Bolton Cross, Brixham, Devon TQ5 8LZ
Tel: (01803) 856267
www.brixhamheritage.org.uk
Local, social maritime history of the fishing port
of Brixham.

Charlestown Shipwreck and Heritage Centre

Quay Road, Charlestown, St Austell, Cornwall
PL25 3NJ
Tel: (01726) 69897
www.shipwreckcharlestown.com
Visual history of Charlestown including life-size
tableaux of former inhabitants, blacksmith and
cooper. Outstanding display of shipwreck material. Diving and RNLI exhibitions.

Dart Pleasure Craft Limited (River Link Operators)

5 Lower Street, Dartmouth, Devon TQ6 9AJ
Tel: (01803) 834488
www.riverlink.co.uk
Five pleasure boats cruising on the River Dart.

Dartmouth Museum

The Butterwalk, Dartmouth, Devon TQ6 9PZ
Tel: (01803) 832923
www.devonmuseums.net/dartmouth
Historic and maritime museum in former merchant's house, dating about 1640. Old photographs and pictures on display, ship models and
ships in bottles.

The Deep Exhibition

The Old Market House, The Quay, Brixham, Devon
TQ5 8AW
Tel: (01803) 858444
An unforgettable nautical adventure exploring
fables, fantasy and local heritage.

The Hardy Monument

Black Down, Portesham, Weymouth, Dorset
Tel: (01297) 561900
www.nationaltrust.org.uk
A monument erected in about 1844, in memory
of Vice-Admiral Sir Thomas Masterman Hardy,
flag captain of HMS *Victory* at the Battle of
Trafalgar.

Hartland Quay Museum

Hartland, Bideford, Devon EX39 6DU
Tel: (01288) 331353
Coastal museum with exhibitions on shipwrecks,
natural history, coastal trades, geology and the

Land's End, Cornwall.

history of Hartland Quay. Superb coastal views
and cliff walks from the museum.

Isles of Scilly Museum

Church Street, St Mary's, Isles of Scilly TR21 0JT
Tel: (01720) 422337
www.iosmuseum.org
All items dealing with the geology, archaeology,
history and natural history of the Isles of Scilly.
Shipwreck material. Library relating to Scilly.

Land's End

The Custom House, Land's End, Sennen,
Penzance, Cornwall TR19 7AA
Tel: (01736) 871501
www.landsend-landmark.co.uk
Spectacular cliffs with breathtaking vistas. Superb
multi-sensory 'Last Labyrinth Show' and other
exhibitions.

Maritime Heritage Centre

Wapping Wharf, Gas Ferry Road, Bristol BS1 6TY
Tel: (0117) 926 0680
Museum introduces the theme of 200 years of
Bristol shipbuilding with particular reference to
Charles Hill & Sons and their predecessor, James
Hilhouse.

Mary Newman's Cottage

48 Culver Road, Saltash, Cornwall PL12 4DT
Childhood home of Mary Newman, the first wife
of Sir Francis Drake. The cottage was probably
built in 1400s, with central passage and pole
staircases to rooms above.

National Maritime Museum Cornwall

Discovery Quay, Falmouth, Cornwall TR11 3QY
Tel: (01326) 313388
www.nmmc.co.uk
Whatever your age or knowledge, this landmark
museum on Falmouth's waterfront is a gateway to
the maritime world, offering unique and interactive displays of boats.

North Devon Maritime Museum

Odun House, Odun Road, Appledore, Bideford,
Devon EX39 1PT
Tel: (01237) 422064
All aspects of North Devon's maritime history
illustrated by models, photographs and paintings.
Interpretation centre for the area and museum.
Video film show. Research room.

Padstow Museum

The Institute, Market Place, Padstow, Cornwall
PL28 8AD
Tel: (01841) 532470 (Chairman at home)
Local museum with only material related to
Padstow and its environs exhibited, including the
Obby Oss custom – one of the oldest surviving
May Day traditions – lifeboat, railway, tools,
domestic artefacts, photographs, shipwrecks.

Pendeen Lighthouse

Pendeen Watch, Pendeen, Penzance, Cornwall
TR19 7ED
Tel: (01209) 210900
Lighthouse tower built in 1900. Engine room
with all original equipment, including the largest
foghorn (sounder) in England.

Tall Ships Race, Falmouth.

Salcombe, Devon.

The Pilchard Works, Newlyn

Tolcarne, Newlyn, Penzance, Cornwall TR18 5QH
Tel: (01736) 332112
www.pilchardworks.co.uk
Cornwall's last working salt pilchard factory,
packing in wooden casks and boxes since about
1905 and now open with three floors of displays
describing Cornwall's fishing heritage.

Portland Castle

CastleTown, Portland, Dorset DT5 1AZ
Tel: (01305) 820539
www.english-heritage.org.uk/portland
A well-preserved coastal fort built by Henry VIII
to defend Weymouth harbour against possible
French and Spanish attack. Exhibition on 400
years of the castle's history.

Quay House Visitor Centre

46 The Quay, Exeter, Devon EX2 4AN
Tel: (01392) 261711
www.exeter.gov.uk/visiting
Restored 17th-century building on Exeter's historic quayside. Static and audio-visual displays
show the growth of this riverside city through the
ages.

Salcombe Maritime and Local History Museum

Town Hall Basement, Market Street, Salcombe,
Devon TQ8 8DE
Tel: (01548) 843080
Local museum featuring exhibits of local mar-
itime interest, shipbuilding, wreck and rescue.
Local history in photographs and artefacts.
Slapton battle-training area display.

SS Great Britain

Great Western Dock, Gas Ferry Road, Bristol
BS1 6TY
Tel: (0117) 926 0680
www.ss-great-britain.com
Designed by Brunel, SS *Great Britain* was the
world's first iron-hulled, screw propeller-driven,
steam-powered passenger liner. She is undergoing
restoration at the Great Western Dock in which
she was built.

Teignmouth and Shaldon Museum

29 French Street, Teignmouth, Devon TQ14 8ST
Tel: (01626) 777041
www.teignmuseum.org.uk
Exhibits include 16th-century cannon and artefacts from the Church Rocks wreck and local history, 1920s pier machines and 1877 cannon.

Trinity House National Lighthouse Centre

Wharf Road, Penzance, Cornwall TR18 4BN
Tel: (01736) 360077
www.lighthousecentre.org.uk
The Trinity House collection of lighthouse and
light vessel artefacts.

WALES

Milford Haven Museum

The Old Custom House, Sybil Way, The Docks,
Milford Haven, Pembrokeshire SA73 3AF
Tel: (01646) 694496
The story of Milford Haven town and waterway
concentrating on the 200- plus years since the
town was founded in 1790.

National Coracle Centre

Cenarth Falls, Cenarth, Newcastle Emlyn,
Ceredigion SA38 9JL
Tel: (01239) 710980
www.coracle-centre.co.uk
A unique collection of coracles including nine
types from Wales and those from many parts of
the world. The workshop area details coracle construction and river demonstrations.

Nelson Museum

Priory Street, Monmouth, Monmouthshire NP5 3XA
Tel: (01600) 713519
A magnificent collection of materials about
Horatio Nelson and a local history collection
about Monmouth and its people, including
Charles Rolls and Henry V.

Rhyl Sea Life Centre

East Parade, Rhyl, Denbighshire LL18 3AF
Tel: (01745) 344660
Over 50 different species of British marine life.

RNLI Lifeboat Museum

Pen-y-Cei, Barmouth, Gwynedd LL42 1HB
Pictorial exhibition of the history of Barmouth
Lifeboat and some models.

NORTHERN IRELAND

Benone Beach

Benone, Limavady County, Londonderry
BT49 0LQ
Seven miles of golden sand backed by sand
dunes and dramatic cliffs and a Martello Tower.
Site of the German submarine fleet surrender.

Harbour Museum

Harbour Square, Londonderry, County
Londonderry BT48 6AF
Tel: (028) 7137 7331
The maritime history of Derry City. Replica of
30-foot curragh in which St Columba sailed to
Iona in AD 563.

Newry Museum

Bank Parade, Newry, County Down BT35 6HP
Tel: (028) 3026 6232
History of the Gap of the North, robes of
the Order of St Patrick, Nelson's table from
HMS *Victory*. Period furniture in a restored
18th-century room.

CHANNEL ISLANDS

Corbiere Lighthouse

Corbiere, St Brelade, Jersey, Channel Islands
This dramatically situated lighthouse on the
south-western corner of the Island was the first
concrete lighthouse in the British Isles.

Fort Grey and Shipwreck Museum

Rocquaine, St Peters, Guernsey, Channel Islands
GY7 9BY
www.museum.guernsey.net
Built in 1804 to defend the Island against invasion, this Martello Tower was restored in 1975
to house a museum on shipwrecks.

Maritime Museum

New North Quay, St Helier, Jersey, Channel
Islands JE2 3ND
www.jerseyheritagetrust.org
The Maritime Museum combines hands-on
exhibits with historic objects and new art and
sculpture to celebrate the centuries-old relationship between islanders and the sea.

Corbiere Lighthouse, Jersey.

Glossary

aftercastle A structure at the stern end of a ship, derived from the freestanding tower-like additions on northern European vessels of the Viking tradition and the raised platforms employed on Mediterranean 'round' ships. Over time the structure became more integrated with the hull topsides, developing into the half-deck, quarterdeck and poop arrangements of carracks and galleons.

Archimedes screw A screw of continuous thread turning inside a cylinder to raise water for purposes of irrigation; its invention was attributed to Archimedes of Syracuse (c. 287–212 BC).

balinger English late medieval craft possibly derived from the clinker-built double-ended craft descended from Viking boats known in the Middle Ages as galleys, i.e. capable of being rowed as well as sailed, as distinct from the sail-only cogs. In the fifteenth century they seem to have been the light scouting and raiding forces of the English navy.

barquentine Nineteenth century term applied to a vessel with a full square-rigged foremast but fore-and-aft rigged main and mizzen. Not so much used for warships, except auxiliary steamers; later some vessels had four or more masts.

bow The foremost part of a ship, beginning where the planks arch inwards, and terminating where they close at the stem or prow.

bowsprit Heavy spar (in effect, a lower mast) angled forward over the bow; provides the support for the foremast stays and allows sail to be set far enough forward to have a significant effect on the balance of the rig.

buss From the fifteenth century, a seagoing fishing vessel with bluff bows, a square stern and a relatively long hull; they were usually rigged with three masts, each with a single square sail, all except one of which were struck when fishing; the one remaining sail gave the vessel enough way to keep the nets taut.

capital ship The largest and most powerful warship types; effectively synonymous with the battleship until the Second World War, latterly the term has been progressively applied to aircraft carriers and more recently nuclear submarines.

carrack The derivation of the word is uncertain: there were small Arab *karaques* in the thirteenth century, and the term may have been passed to the West via Muslim influence in Iberia, but the ship type seems to owe nothing to Arab craft. The carrack was developed as a compromise between the typical square rig of the northern European nations and the lateen rig of the Mediterranean. It seems to have acquired more sail from quite early, a Catalan contract of 1353 specifying main and mizzen, and the English captured a number of two-masters from the Genoese early in the fifteenth century. By the middle of the 1400s three-masted examples were known and the multi-decked forestage and aftercastle were becoming more marked. With the application of the hull-mounted gunport, carracks became the capital ships of the sixteenth-century navies, until superseded in the latter half of the century by the galleon.

centreline Imaginary vertical plane drawn along the ship from stem to stern.

clipper Generally denoting a fine-lined, fast sailing vessel.

cog The classic sailing ship of northern Europe in the high Middle Ages, the cog was developed on the Frisian coast from whence its usage spread down the North Sea coasts and into the Baltic before reaching the Mediterranean. Its capacious flat-bottomed form, with straight raked stem and stern posts, is believed to derive from the technology of the logboat, but by the thirteenth century, the type had evolved into a seagoing vessel of several hundred tons in its largest form. It acquitted a stern rudder on the centreline to replace the steering oars and was powered by a single square sail.

coracle Small boat usually associated with the Celtic areas of Britain, constructed of wickerwork and originally covered with hides but more recently pitch or tarred canvas has been used. The Welsh version is usually small and round (or a rounded rectangle) in shape, man-portable and designed to carry one or, at most, two people, usually for fishing on rivers and lakes. The Irish version is larger, more boat-like, and very seaworthy.

fireship A vessel either converted or purpose-built to be expended as a floating incendiary device; special fittings enabled the fireship to be ignited at the last moment, thus allowing the crew a chance of escaping by boat before collision with the target.

first rate Always the largest ships of the fleet, of 100 guns or more, but the lower end of the spectrum varied in British practice from 60 guns in 1651 to 80 guns in the 1660s and 100 guns after about 1700.

flag of convenience A national flag flown by a ship registered in that country to gain financial or legal advantage.

fore-and-aft The lengthway of the ship.

forecastle Structure at the bow of a ship, derived from the free-standing tower like additions on northern European vessels of the Viking tradition and the raised platforms employed on Mediterranean 'round' ships. Over time the design became more integrated with the hull topsides, developing into the multi-decked defensible structures of carracks and galleons.

freeboard Height from upper deck to waterline. If freeboard is too low, the ship will be wet and may lack stability at large angles of heel.

furl To wrap or roll a sail close to the yard, stay, or mast to which it belongs, and secure a gasket or cord about it to fasten it thereto.

gaff A short spar to extend the head of a fore-and-aft sail; usually hoisted with the sail, for which purpose it was equipped with jaws that fitted around the mast.

keel (i) The lowermost longitudinal structural member of the hull; in effect, its 'backbone', the frames forming the 'ribs'. (ii) In the north-east of England a type of barge for river use, usually propelled by one large sail.

ketch A two-masted rig characterised by a main and mizzen (often said to be a ship rig without a foremast); originally square rigged, but fore-and-aft versions became common later.

lateen Triangular sail set from a long yard

that was slung from its mast at an approximate 45-degree angle; any kind of vessel whose principal driving sails were of this kind was said to be lateen rigged. The rig is ancient in origin and was employed by galleys and most kinds of Mediterranean war vessels; the sail also formed the mizzen course of square riggers until the late eighteenth century.

port Name given by seamen for the left side of the ship, when looking forward from the stern (replaced the term larboard abolished in 1844). Also the order to put the helm over to the larboard side of the ship.

quarterdeck A deck covering the after end of the uppermost complete deck; the area from which the officers controlled the ship.

red ensign The ensign originally used to denote the senior squadron of the English fleet. When the division of red, white, and blue squadrons was abolished in 1864, the red ensign, informally known as the red duster, became the ensign of the British merchant fleet and is today flown by all British merchant vessels.

reef To reduce a sail by tying a portion of it to the yards with points.

square rig Any sail plan in which the principal power was derived from canvas set from yards that crossed the centreline of the ship (the yards were 'square' – at right angles – to the centreline when the wind was directly aft).

starboard The right side of the ship, when the eye of the spectator is directed forward or towards the head.

sternpost The near-vertical extension of the keel aft on which the rudder was hung; the principal element in the construction of the stern.

tack To change the course from one board to another or to turn the ship about from the starboard to the larboard tack, or vice versa, in a contrary wind. Also, to make way to windward by carrying out several tacks.

yard A spar crossing a mast from which a sail is set. Horizontally set yards, which are primarily oriented athwartship are for square sails; those at an angle and set in the fore-and-aft line are called lateens if they cross the mast, or gaffs if they are set aft of it.

Picture Credits

Bridgeman Art Library /www.bridgeman.co.uk 22T Museum of London, 26 Bibliothèque Nationale /Paris, 150 Joseph Mallord William Turner (1775-1851) British Museum; www.britainonview.com BC C, 2/3, 8, 9, 11, 13, 14, 15, 36T, 36B, 44T, 51B, 80, 88BL, 124, 128, 129, 132, 133, 135T, 147; ©Copyright The Trustees of The British Museum 16/17, 20T, 20CL, 20CR, 20BR; The British Waterways Photo Library 44B; Chrysalis Image Library 56, 72, 77T, 94, 97, 101, 102, 103, 104T, 104B, 112, 113, 118, 122T, 126B, 134, 138, 142, 145B, 155, 156, 157, 158, 160; Chatham Historic Dockyard Trust/ www.chdt.org.uk 60, 120, 143; Corbis FC T Robert Estall, 21 Sean Sexton Collection, 22B Ted Splegel, 23 Nik Wheeler, 24 Archivo Iconografico S.A., 162 Richard Townshend; Philip Springthorpe /Cutty Sark Trust www.cuttysark.org.uk 51T; DPPI/ Vincent Curuchet 7; Dundee Heritage Trust, www.rrsdiscovery.com 63 T&B; The Excelsior Trust 99; Geoff Hunt RSMA 105, 151; Martin Phillips 48; ©Museum of London 19; ©The Mary Rose Trust 32 T&B; ©Ron McCormick 25; Norwich Castle Museum & Art Gallery FC B; National Maritime Museum (ref. Numbers included) FC BL (BHC3384), SPINE (B4919), BC L (BHC4167), BC R (BHC1572), 1 (BHC4126), 6 (BHC0565), 18T (C1240), 18B (D1792), 27T (B4919), 27C (B4927), 29 (C6263-1), 30/31 (BHC0262), 31B (D3296), 33 (BHC0292), 34 (BHC1782), 35 (D7791), 38/39 (BHC0549), 40/41 (BHC0552), 42/43 (PX9696), 45 (D4725), 47 (D4695), 49 (D7528-2), 50 (D6169-3), 52 (D4677), 54/55 (BHC1873), 57 (BHC4227), 59 (BHC1935), 61 (PW6032), 62 (D2184), 64/65 (P8236), 66T (PX8527), 66B (PU7765), 67 (PW4974), 68 (BHC1558), 69 (PW4236), 70 (N61520), 71 (BHC1823), 73 (AD26510), 74 (BHC3756), 75 (BHC0619), 76 (PY0923), 77B (BHC3384), 79 (BHC0636), 82 (BHC3172), 85 (PW1230), 86/87 (D6783-1), 88 BR (D3161-1), 89 (F0256), 90 (PZ5425), 92 (D7562), 93 (PU8484), 95 (PU0976), 96 (BHC1572), 98 (D4456-10), 106/107 (F3201), 106B (A2942), 108 (B9460), 109 (BHC2379), 110L (A2885), 110R (G10892), 114/115 (BHC2369), 115 (PY7410), 116/117 (BHC0993), 120/121 (PY0199), 121T (F2843-1), 122B (PU6772), 125 (BHC0891), 126T (BHC1196), 130 (E0228-1), 131 (B446-2), 136/137 (BHC1554), 140/141 (BHC0672-1), 144 (BHC1555), 145T (BHC1577), 146 (BHC0689), 148/149 (BHC1022), 153 (D7360-1), 153B (D7360-2), 154 (B3822); By kind permission of The P&O Art Collection 111; Port of Felixstowe 158/159; ©Royal Navy/Crown Copyright 161; Courtesy of the RYA 135B; ©The Royal Yacht Britannia 127; Southampton City Council 28; Southampton City Heritage Services 119; Scottish Fisheries Museum 100; Scottish Maritime Museum 91L&R; SS Great Britain Trust 78L&R; Tony Treger, Arbroath 123; Tyne & Wear Museums 83C John Bowes leaving the Tyne: by Frank Mason ©The Laing Art Gallery, 83B The Mayor's Barge on the Tyne: Ascension Day: by J W Carmichael ©The Laing Art Gallery; Yorkshire Tourist Board 58.

Bibliography

Automobile Association, *Illustrated Guide to Britain's Coast*, London, 1984.

Barnett, Corelli, *Engage the Enemy More Closely*, London, 1991.

Brouwer, Norman J, *The International Register of Historic Ships*, London, 1999.

Brown, D K, *Nelson to Vanguard*, London, 2000.

Carr Laughton, L G, *Old Ship Figureheads and Sterns*, 1925, reprinted London 1991.

Casson, Lionel, *Ships and Seafaring in Ancient Times*, London, 1994.

Chapman, Fredrik Hendrik af, *Architectura Navalis Mercatoria*, reprinted London *c*. 1970.

Coad, Jonathan, *The Royal Dockyards 1690–1850*, London, 1989.

Cordingly, David, *Marine Painting in England*, London, 1974.

Corlett, Ewen, *The Iron Ship*, London, 1975.

Coull, James R, *The Sea Fisheries of Scotland*, Edinburgh, 1996.

Davis, Ralph, *The Rise of the English Shipping Industry in the 17th and 18th Centuries*, Newton Abbot, 1962.

Fox, Frank, *Great Ships*, London, 1980.

Friel, Ian, *Maritime History of Britain and Ireland*, London, 2003.

Clifton, Gloria and Rigby, Nigel, *Treasures of the National Maritime Museum*, Greenwich, 2004.

Greenhill, Basil (ed.), *The Advent of Steam*, London, 1993.

Greenhill, Basil and Mannering, Julian (eds), *The Chatham Directory of Inshore Craft*, London, 1997.

Grove, Eric, *Vanguard to Trident*, London, 1987.

Halpern, Paul G, *A Naval History of World War I*, London, 1994.

Hope, Ronald, *A New History of British Shipping*, London, 1990.

Howarth, David and Stephen, *The Story of P&O*, London, 1994.

Hutchison, Gillian, *Medieval Ships and Shipping*, London, 1994.

Jackson, Gordon, *The History and Archaeology of Ports*, Tadworth, 1983.

Kirkaldy, A W, *British Shipping, its History, Organisation and Importance*, 1914, reprinted Newton Abbot 1970.

Lambert, Andrew, *The Last Sailing Battlefleet*, London, 1991.

Lambert, Andrew (ed.), *Steam, Steel and Shellfire*, London, 1992.

Lavery, Brian, *Nelson's Navy*, London, 1989.

Lavery, Brian, *Maritime Scotland*, London, 2001.

Lavery, Brian, *Ship*, London, 2004.

Lavery, Brian with Stephens, Simon, *Ship Models*, London, 1996.

Lyon, David, *The Sailing Navy List*, London, 1993.

McGrail, Sean, *Boats of the World*, Oxford, 2004.

McKnight, Hugh, *The Shell Book of Inland Waterways*, Newton Abbot, 1975.

Martin, Colin and Parker, Geoffrey, *The Spanish Armada*, London, 1988.

Milne, Gustav, *The Port of Roman London*, London, 1985.

Paine, Lincoln, *Ships of the World*, London, 1998.

Phillips-Birt, Douglas, *The History of Yachting*, London, 1974.

Platt, Colin, *Medieval Southampton, the Port and Trading Community*, London, 1973.

Pollard, Sidney and Robertson, Paul, *The British Shipbuilding Industry, 1870-1914*, Cambridge Massachusetts and London, 1979.

Ritchie-Noakes, Nancy, *Liverpool's Historic Waterfront*, London, 1984.

Robinson, Adrian and Millward, Roy, *The Shell Book of the British Coast*, Newton Abbot, 1983.

Rodger, N A M, *The Wooden World*, London, 1986.

Rodger, N A M, *The Safeguard of the Sea*, London, 1997.

Rodger, N A M, *The Command of the Ocean*, London, 2004.

Rule, Margaret, *The Mary Rose*, London, 1982.

Sobel, Dava, *Longitude*, London, 1996.

Sumida, Jon Tetsuro, *In Defence of Naval Supremacy*, London, 1989.

Index